REALSIMPLE
meals made easy

WRITTEN BY RENEE SCHETTLER
PHOTOGRAPHS BY ANNA WILLIAMS

REALSIMPLE Oxmoor House.

...YOU'VE NO DOUBT HEARD THE ADAGE about the unavoidable nature of death and taxes. To that short, onerous list I'd like to add one more thing: making dinner. Even for those of us who like to cook, the routine inevitability of dinner can feel...oppressive. And unlike death and taxes, dinner is something you experience every night. Rain or shine, in good times and bad, accompanied by soft music or the clatter of a baby spoon on a high-chair tray, dinnertime will eventually be upon you. You may be ready, and you may not.

With that in mind, can you think of a more appealing phrase than "easy dinner"? Probably not, considering you've picked up this book. And easy dinner is just what this book delivers. Whether you're looking for a meal that can go from oven to table in 30 minutes (or less), or one that requires very little cleanup (think one pot) or no stove (really), you can turn to any of the seven chapters in this book and know that, regardless of what type of night you're having, supper will be solved.

Although the recipes in this collection of *Real Simple* favorites may promise different benefits—after all, there aren't many dishes that both require no cooking and freeze well—they share certain key attributes. They have been rigorously tested, meaning they are easy to follow and virtually foolproof by the time they make it to your kitchen. They take readily available ingredients and combine them in fresh, unexpected ways. And because the ingredients are familiar (read: widely acceptable to all ages), they will be sure to please just about any palate.

I HOPE YOU FIND THIS BOOK a stress-reducing (not to mention beautiful) addition to your kitchen. It will not render death, taxes, or even making dinner avoidable, but it will turn that last activity into something you can actually look forward to. Every day.

KRISTIN VAN OGTROP
Managing Editor, *Real Simple*

contents

one-pot meals

Sometimes preparing dinner can feel like conducting a symphony…on your stovetop. While a motley crew of cookware simultaneously sautés, boils, and stews, you struggle to keep it all in tune. And your reward after the performance? A sinkful of dirty dishes. Perhaps it's time you introduced a few solo acts into your repertoire. The recipes in this chapter require only a single pot, pan, or skillet, making it particularly easy to pull off a flawless performance. Better still, you can leave what minimal cleanup there is to your little percussionists.

ROAST CHICKEN AND VEGETABLES

hands-on time: 30 minutes | total time: 2 hours | makes 4 servings

1 3¹/₂ - to 4-pound chicken

2 teaspoons kosher salt

¹/₂ teaspoon black pepper

2 lemons, halved

1 cup fresh herbs (parsley, tarragon, thyme, rosemary, or sage, in any combination)

3 tablespoons unsalted butter, at room temperature

3 medium yellow onions, cut into ¹/₂-inch-thick slices

3 carrots, peeled (and halved lengthwise, if thick)

1¹/₂ pounds Yukon gold or new potatoes, halved (if small) or cut into 1¹/₂-inch chunks (peel first, if desired)

1 head garlic, unpeeled

Heat oven to 425° F. Rinse the chicken inside and out and pat it dry with paper towels. Season the inside with ¹/₂ teaspoon of the salt and ¹/₄ teaspoon of the pepper. Place the lemons and herbs inside the cavity. Rub the outside of the bird with the butter and season with ¹/₂ teaspoon of the salt and the remaining pepper. Place the onions, carrots, potatoes, and garlic in a roasting pan. Season with the remaining salt. Place the chicken on top of the vegetables and roast until the thigh registers 180° F on a meat thermometer, about 1¹/₂ hours. Let the chicken rest on a cutting board for 15 minutes before carving. Meanwhile, using a slotted spoon, transfer the onions, carrots, and potatoes to a platter. Using a large spoon, skim any fat from the surface of the pan juices and discard. Place the roasting pan over medium heat and simmer the pan juices until slightly reduced, about 3 minutes. Transfer the chicken to the platter and serve the pan juices on the side.

••• Tip

If you don't have a roasting pan, use a large ovenproof skillet to roast the chicken. (It's also the perfect size and shape for deep-dish apple pie.)

one-pot meals

BEEF AND BEER STEW

hands-on time: 25 minutes | total time: 3 hours, 15 minutes | makes 6 servings

6 tablespoons olive oil

4 slices bacon, diced

2 1/2 pounds rump roast or bottom
round, cut into 6 equal portions, or
2 1/2 pounds precut stew meat

1/2 teaspoon kosher salt

1/4 teaspoon black pepper

4 medium yellow onions, thickly sliced

2 cloves garlic, crushed

1 14.5-ounce can diced tomatoes

2 12-ounce bottles dark beer,
such as brown ale

2 tablespoons light brown sugar

1 tablespoon minced fresh thyme
or 1 teaspoon dried thyme

1 tablespoon minced fresh rosemary
or 1 teaspoon dried rosemary

1 1/2 pounds Yukon gold potatoes,
cut into 1 1/2-inch chunks
(peel first, if desired)

Heat oven to 350° F. Place the oil and bacon in a Dutch oven over medium heat. Fry the bacon until crisp and transfer it to a paper towel–lined plate; set aside. Season the beef with the salt and pepper. Add some of the beef to the pot, being careful not to crowd the pieces. Cook until browned, about 7 minutes per side. Transfer to the plate with the bacon; set aside. Repeat with the remaining beef. Add the onions and garlic to the pot and cook until softened, about 7 minutes. Spoon off and discard any excess fat. Return the beef and bacon to the pot and add the tomatoes, beer, brown sugar, thyme, and rosemary. Bring to a simmer. Cover and transfer to oven. After 10 minutes, check to see if the stew is simmering; if not, increase oven temperature by 25° F. Cook until the meat is falling apart, about 2 hours. Add the potatoes and cook until tender, about 30 minutes more. To serve, ladle the stew into individual bowls.

••• Tip

A Dutch oven may be old-fashioned, but it's not outdated. Use this ovenproof pot with a tight-fitting lid for stews, roasts, braises, and baked beans.

SCALLOP AND CORN CHOWDER

hands-on time: 25 minutes | total time: 50 minutes | makes 4 servings

5 slices bacon

1 1/2 pounds sea scallops (about 16)

3/4 teaspoon kosher salt

1/4 teaspoon black pepper

1 small yellow onion, thinly sliced into half-moons

1/2 pound Yukon gold potatoes, cut into 1/2-inch pieces (peel first, if desired)

1/2 cup dry white wine

1 cup low-sodium chicken broth

1/2 cup heavy cream

1 cup corn kernels, frozen or fresh (from 2 ears)

1/4 cup finely chopped fresh flat-leaf parsley leaves

Fry the bacon in a large skillet or stockpot over medium heat until crisp. Transfer to a paper towel–lined plate; set aside. You should have about 2 tablespoons of bacon drippings remaining in the pan (if not, supplement with olive oil). Rinse the scallops and pat them dry with paper towels. Season them with the salt and pepper. Increase heat to medium-high. Add some of the scallops to the pan, being careful not to crowd them. Cook until golden brown, about 2 minutes per side. Transfer to a plate. Repeat with the remaining scallops. Reduce heat to medium. Add the onion to the pan and cook until softened, about 5 minutes. Add the potatoes, wine, broth, and cream. Bring to a simmer. Cover partially and simmer gently until the potatoes are tender, about 20 minutes. Add the scallops and corn and cook for 4 minutes. To serve, ladle into bowls and sprinkle with the parsley and crumbled bacon.

••• Tip

What's the main difference between sea scallops and bay scallops? Their size and origin: Big sea scallops come from the open ocean, while small bay scallops hail from closer to shore.

one-pot meals

VEGETABLE SOUP

hands-on time: 20 minutes | total time: 40 minutes | makes 4 servings

2 tablespoons olive oil

1 large yellow onion, chopped

2 carrots, chopped

2 celery stalks, chopped

3 14.5-ounce cans low-sodium
  chicken broth

1/2 pound Yukon gold potatoes,
  cut into 1-inch chunks
  (peel first, if desired)

1 tablespoon fresh thyme leaves
  or 1 teaspoon dried thyme

1/2 teaspoon kosher salt

1 14.5-ounce can diced tomatoes

1/4 pound green beans, cut into
  1-inch pieces

1 cup chopped broccoli
  Grated Parmesan (optional)

1 baguette, sliced and toasted
  (optional)

Heat the oil in a large saucepan or stockpot over medium-high heat. Add the onion, carrots, and celery and cook until softened but not browned, about 5 minutes. Add the broth, 1 cup of water, the potatoes, thyme, and salt. Bring to a boil. Reduce heat, cover partially, and simmer for 15 minutes. Add the tomatoes, beans, and broccoli, return to a simmer, and cook until the vegetables are tender, 5 to 10 minutes. To serve, ladle the soup into bowls. Sprinkle with the Parmesan and serve with the baguette slices, if desired.

and the next time, try...
Making an ad hoc minestrone. When you add the potatoes to the pot, also include one 15-ounce can of cannellini beans (drained), 1/2 a head of cabbage (shredded), and a handful of macaroni or broken spaghetti.

•••Tip
When it comes to cooking, the gold standard of potatoes is, well, the Yukon gold. Not only does it have a rich, buttery flavor but it also retains its shape during heating, making it terrific for soups, stews, roasts, and mashes.

ROAST COD WITH CRISP POTATOES

hands-on time: 10 minutes | total time: 50 minutes | makes 6 servings

3 pounds Yukon gold or new potatoes, halved (if small) or cut into 1$\frac{1}{2}$-inch chunks (peel first, if desired)

3 tablespoons plus 2 teaspoons olive oil

1 teaspoon kosher salt

$\frac{1}{2}$ teaspoon black pepper

6 6-ounce cod fillets, skin removed

Zest of $\frac{1}{2}$ lemon, peeled into thin strips (optional)

1 tablespoon chopped fresh chives (optional)

Heat oven to 450° F. Place the potatoes in a roasting pan or on a baking sheet. Drizzle with 3 tablespoons of the oil and toss to coat. Sprinkle with $\frac{1}{2}$ teaspoon of the salt and $\frac{1}{4}$ teaspoon of the pepper. Roast for 20 minutes. Stir and roast for 10 minutes more. Meanwhile, rinse the cod fillets and pat them dry with paper towels. After the 30 minutes of roasting, move the potatoes to the sides of the pan and place the fillets in the center. Drizzle with the remaining oil and sprinkle with the remaining salt and pepper. Redistribute the potatoes around the fillets. Roast until the fillets are the same color throughout and flake easily, about 10 minutes. Top with the lemon zest and chives (if using).

•••Tip

Serve this baked version of fish and chips along with ketchup for the kids and malt vinegar for the adults.

one-pot meals

LAMB TAGINE WITH COUSCOUS

hands-on time: 50 minutes | total time: 2 hours (includes marinating) | makes 6 to 8 servings

2 teaspoons paprika

1/4 teaspoon ground turmeric

1/2 teaspoon ground cumin

1/4 teaspoon ground cayenne

1 teaspoon ground cinnamon

1 teaspoon kosher salt

4 tablespoons olive oil

1 1/2 pounds lamb loin, cut into
1 1/2-inch pieces

1 yellow onion, thickly sliced

4 carrots, peeled into thin strips

1 clove garlic, finely chopped

1 tablespoon grated fresh ginger
Zest of 1/2 lemon, grated

1 32-ounce container low-sodium
chicken broth

1 10-ounce box couscous

1/4 cup fresh cilantro leaves,
roughly chopped

1/4 cup fresh flat-leaf parsley leaves,
roughly chopped

1/4 cup kalamata olives, pitted
and halved

Combine the paprika, turmeric, cumin, cayenne, cinnamon, salt, and 2 tablespoons of the oil in a large resealable bag. Add the lamb, seal, and shake to coat. Refrigerate for at least 1 hour and up to 12. Heat the remaining oil in a large saucepan or Dutch oven over medium heat. Add the onion and carrots. Cook, stirring occasionally, for 15 minutes. Transfer to a plate. Add some of the lamb to the pan, being careful not to crowd the pieces. Brown on all sides, about 12 minutes total. Transfer to a plate. Repeat with the remaining lamb. Return all the lamb to the pot. Add the garlic, ginger, and lemon zest and stir to coat. Return the onion and carrots to the pot, add the broth, and bring to a boil. Stir in the couscous. Remove from heat, cover, and let rest for 10 minutes. Stir in the cilantro, parsley, and olives. Divide among individual bowls.

and the next time, try...

Cutting the cooking time in half by using leftover chicken or turkey. Instead of coating the meat with the spices, just add the spices to the oil with the garlic, ginger, and zest. Then add the meat when you stir in the couscous.

••• Tip

If you can't find loin of lamb, ask your butcher to cut a leg of lamb into 1 1/2-inch pieces. Although relatively expensive, these cuts cook quickly and are very tender.

BAKED BEANS

hands-on time: 15 minutes | total time: 17 hours (includes soaking) | makes 6 to 8 servings

1 pound dry navy or soldier beans

1/3 cup molasses

1/3 cup cider vinegar

1 teaspoon dry mustard

1/2 cup dark brown sugar,
firmly packed

1/4 teaspoon black pepper

1 large white onion, quartered

1/4 pound salt pork or bacon, cut into
1 1/2-inch chunks
Buttered bread, such as Boston
brown or a hearty whole-grain,
for serving

Place the beans in a large ovenproof pot or Dutch oven. Add enough water to cover by 3 inches and let stand for at least 10 hours. Drain the beans and return them to the pot. Add just enough water to cover the beans. Bring to a boil, then reduce heat and simmer gently until the beans are softened, about 1 hour. (Add water periodically as necessary to keep the beans barely covered.) Meanwhile, in a medium bowl, whisk together the molasses, vinegar, mustard, brown sugar, pepper, and 2 tablespoons of water. Drain the beans. Place the onion in the empty pot. Top with the beans, then the salt pork or bacon, then the molasses mixture. Heat oven to 300° F. Cover the pot tightly and bake until the beans are tender, the bacon is falling apart, and the liquid is thick and bubbling, about 6 hours. Check the beans during the last hour of cooking; if they appear to be drying out, add more water (or even a second batch of the molasses mixture). Spoon the beans into individual bowls and serve with the buttered bread.

••• Tip

Salt pork is similar to bacon—it's just thicker, fattier, and unsmoked. Look for it near the bacon in the supermarket.

one-pot meals

ROAST SALMON, FENNEL, AND RED ONION

hands-on time: 10 minutes | total time: 45 minutes | makes 4 servings

2 small fennel bulbs, cut into
  $1/2$-inch wedges

1 large red onion, cut into
  $1/2$-inch wedges

6 cloves garlic

1 cup cherry or grape tomatoes

$1/2$ bunch fresh thyme sprigs

1 teaspoon kosher salt

$1/2$ teaspoon black pepper

2 teaspoons olive oil

4 6-ounce salmon fillets, skin
  removed

1 lemon, halved

Heat oven to 400° F. Place the fennel, onion, garlic, tomatoes, thyme sprigs, $1/2$ teaspoon of the salt, $1/4$ teaspoon of the pepper, and the oil in a roasting pan or 9-by-13-inch baking dish and toss to coat. Spread evenly and roast for 20 minutes. Meanwhile, rinse the salmon fillets and pat them dry with paper towels. Move the vegetables to the sides of the pan and place the fillets in the center. Redistribute the vegetables around the fillets. Squeeze the lemon over the top, then sprinkle with the remaining salt and pepper. Return to oven and roast until the fillets are the same color throughout and flake easily, about 10 to 12 minutes. To serve, transfer the fillets and vegetables to individual plates.

••• Tip

To remove burnt-on food from a roasting pan or a baking dish, add a generous pinch of baking soda before filling it with warm water. Then set it aside to soak for at least 1 hour before washing.

CHICKEN CACCIATORE

hands-on time: 45 minutes | total time: 1 hour, 50 minutes | makes 4 servings

1/4 cup all-purpose flour

1 1/4 teaspoons kosher salt

3/4 teaspoon black pepper

1 3 1/2- to 4-pound chicken, cut into pieces

1/4 cup olive oil

1 medium yellow onion, roughly chopped

1 carrot, diced

1 celery stalk, diced

4 cloves garlic, finely chopped

3 sprigs fresh thyme

1 bay leaf

1 28-ounce can plum tomatoes

1/3 cup dry red wine

1/4 cup chopped fresh flat-leaf parsley leaves

In a shallow bowl, combine the flour, 1 teaspoon of the salt, and 1/2 teaspoon of the pepper. Rinse the chicken and pat it dry with paper towels. Working in batches, lightly coat the chicken in the flour mixture, shaking off any excess. Heat the oil in a Dutch oven or large saucepan over medium heat. Add some of the chicken to the pan, being careful not to crowd the pieces. Cook the chicken until browned, 4 to 5 minutes per side. Transfer to a plate; set aside. Repeat with the remaining chicken. Add the onion to the pan and cook for 2 minutes. Add the carrot, celery, garlic, thyme, and bay leaf. Cook, stirring occasionally, for 10 minutes. Crush the tomatoes in the can with a large spoon and stir them into the vegetables. Add the wine and the remaining salt and pepper and bring to a simmer. Add the chicken, reduce heat, and cover. Simmer for 45 minutes, turning the pieces occasionally. Remove and discard the bay leaf. Stir in the parsley and serve on individual plates.

•••Tip

If you have a difficult time adjusting the flame on your stovetop so it maintains a gentle simmer, try stacking two burner grates, one on top of the other (just make absolutely sure that one fits securely over the other and that they are stable and level). The second grate will act as a buffer for a flame that is a little too hot.

one-pot meals

CREAMY PARMESAN RISOTTO

hands-on time: 40 minutes | total time: 45 minutes | makes 4 servings

4 tablespoons unsalted butter

1 medium yellow onion,
  finely chopped

1 clove garlic, finely chopped

1½ cups Arborio rice

1 cup dry white wine

4 cups low-sodium chicken broth

½ teaspoon kosher salt

¼ teaspoon black pepper

½ cup (2 ounces) grated Parmesan,
  plus more for serving

Melt 2 tablespoons of the butter in a medium saucepan over medium heat. Add the onion and garlic and cook, stirring with a wooden spoon, until the onion is softened, about 5 minutes. Add the rice and cook, stirring constantly, until it is coated with butter and begins to turn translucent, about 2 minutes. Add the wine and cook, stirring frequently, until all the liquid is absorbed, 3 to 5 minutes. Meanwhile, pour the broth into a medium bowl and microwave on high until hot but not boiling. Ladle ½ cup of the warm broth into the rice mixture. Simmer, stirring occasionally, until the broth is absorbed. Repeat, adding ½ cup of the broth at a time, until the rice is cooked through but still firm. This should take 20 to 25 minutes total (you may need to reheat the broth once during this time). Remove from heat and add the salt, pepper, Parmesan, and the remaining butter. Stir to combine. Serve immediately with additional Parmesan on the side.

••• Tip

Contrary to common kitchen lore, it's not necessary to stir risotto constantly. Frequent stirring is required at the beginning to coax the rice to creaminess. But after you've added the first ladleful or two of broth, an occasional stir will suffice.

STEAMED HALIBUT AND ASPARAGUS IN PARCHMENT

hands-on time: 25 minutes │ total time: 50 minutes │ makes 4 servings

1¹/₂ pounds small red potatoes,
    sliced about ¹/₄ inch thick

4 6-ounce halibut fillets, skin removed

2 teaspoons kosher salt

1 teaspoon black pepper

2 tablespoons chopped fresh tarragon

4 scallions, trimmed and cut
    into 1-inch pieces

1 pound asparagus, trimmed and
    cut into 1-inch pieces

1 tablespoon extra-virgin olive oil

Parchment paper, cut into
8 15-by-15-inch sheets

Heat oven to 400° F. Divide 4 of the parchment paper sheets between 2 baking sheets. (The paper sheets may overlap slightly.) Place ¹/₄ of the potatoes in the center of each sheet. Rinse the halibut fillets and pat them dry with paper towels. Place the fillets on top of the potatoes. Season with the salt and pepper. Add the tarragon, scallions, and asparagus. Drizzle with the oil. Top with the remaining parchment paper sheets and fold the edges over several times to seal. Bake for 25 minutes. (Although you can't check for doneness, this is ample time for the fish and potatoes to cook through.) To serve, place a packet on each plate and cut open.

and the next time, try...
Using almost anything that swims in place of the halibut. Salmon, tuna, and cod all work just fine and cook in about the same amount of time.

••• Tip

If the folded edge of a parchment packet starts to unfold, place half a lemon or a carrot on the offending seam to keep it flat while baking.

one-pot meals

ROAST CHICKEN WITH OLIVES AND THYME

hands-on time: 25 minutes | total time: 2 hours, 25 minutes (includes marinating) | makes 4 servings

1 3 1/2- to 4-pound chicken,
   cut into pieces
1 teaspoon honey
1 small shallot, finely chopped
1/2 cup extra-virgin olive oil
1 1/2 teaspoons kosher salt
1 teaspoon black pepper
   Zest of 1 lemon, peeled in
   thin strips
1/4 cup fresh lemon juice
1 cup kalamata olives, pitted
5 cloves garlic, thinly sliced
1 small bunch fresh thyme sprigs
1 small head cauliflower, cut into
   florets (optional)

Rinse the chicken and pat it dry with paper towels. Place it in a roasting pan or 9-by-13-inch baking dish. In a small bowl, combine the honey, shallot, oil, 1 teaspoon of the salt, 1/4 teaspoon of the pepper, lemon zest and juice, olives, and garlic. Pour the lemon mixture over the chicken and turn to coat. Scatter the thyme sprigs over the top. Refrigerate, covered, for at least 1 hour or overnight. Heat oven to 425° F. Season the chicken with the remaining salt and pepper. Place the cauliflower (if using) around the chicken and spoon the lemon mixture over the top. Roast until the chicken is golden brown, about 20 minutes. Reduce heat to 375° F. Continue to roast until the chicken is cooked through, about 40 minutes more. Spoon the olives and pan juices over the chicken and serve.

••• Tip

Roasting chicken pieces, as opposed to an entire chicken, takes slightly less time and spares you the hassle of carving.

CHAPTER TWO

no-shop meals

It's your third time scavenging through the fridge, the freezer, and the cabinets, helplessly hoping that *something* will materialize for dinner and spare you a trip to the store. Yet all you've turned up is a box of pasta, a stray jalapeño, and one-sixteenth of a bag of frozen peas. Not exactly the makings of a proper meal—or so it would appear. Next time you need to conjure something out of nothing, take a quick inventory of the recipes on the following pages. Then check the pantry again. Dinner is in there, if you know where to look.

FLUFFY CORN AND GOAT CHEESE OMELETS

hands-on time: 25 minutes | total time: 30 minutes | makes 2 servings

6 eggs, separated
1/2 teaspoon kosher salt
1/4 teaspoon black pepper
1 cup corn kernels, frozen or fresh (from 2 ears)
2 tablespoons unsalted butter
1/2 cup (2 ounces) goat cheese, crumbled
8 fresh chives, chopped

In a large bowl, whisk together the egg yolks, salt, pepper, and corn. In a separate bowl, using an electric mixer on medium, beat the egg whites until soft peaks form. With a spatula, gently fold the egg whites into the yolk mixture until no trace of white remains. Melt 1 tablespoon of the butter in a nonstick skillet over medium heat. Pour in half of the egg mixture. Cook, without stirring, until the eggs barely begin to set, about 1 minute. Use the spatula to lift the edge of the omelet so the uncooked egg flows underneath. Cook, still without stirring, until the top is almost completely set, about 2 minutes. Sprinkle 1/3 of the cheese and 1/3 of the chives over half the omelet. Using the spatula, fold the other half of the omelet over the filling. Cook until set. Tilt the skillet and slide the omelet onto a plate. Repeat with the remaining butter, egg mixture, and half the remaining cheese and chives. Sprinkle the omelets with the remaining cheese and chives. Serve immediately.

••• Tip

When you cook omelets, use a skillet that doesn't have a plastic or wooden handle. That way, if the eggs are still runny on top but are beginning to brown on the bottom, you can stick the skillet under the broiler for about 30 seconds to set the eggs before folding the omelet.

no-shop meals

TUNA AND WHITE BEAN SALAD

hands-on time: 15 minutes | total time: 15 minutes | makes 4 servings

2 6-ounce cans tuna, drained
1 15-ounce can cannellini beans, drained and rinsed
1 12-ounce jar roasted red peppers, drained and roughly chopped
2 tablespoons capers
Zest of 1 lemon, grated
1 tomato, roughly chopped (optional)
3 tablespoons fresh lemon juice
1 tablespoon extra-virgin olive oil
1/2 teaspoon kosher salt
1/2 teaspoon black pepper
Toasted bread, such as pita, for serving

In a large bowl, combine the tuna, beans, red peppers, capers, lemon zest, and tomato (if using). In a separate bowl, whisk together the lemon juice, oil, salt, and black pepper. Pour the vinaigrette over the tuna mixture and toss. Serve with the bread.

and the next time, try...
Improvising with whatever kitchen staples you have on hand:
• Olives
• Red onion
• Chickpeas
• Celery
• Fresh basil or flat-leaf parsley
• Jarred artichokes
• Balsamic vinegar
• Cooked rice

•••Tip
Stash a couple of cans of Italian tuna packed in olive oil in your cabinet for emergencies. The tuna's robust—but not tinny—taste makes it a great go-to for salads, sandwiches, and pasta dishes.

PARMESAN-CRUSTED CHICKEN CUTLETS

hands-on time: 20 minutes | total time: 30 minutes | makes 4 servings

2 large eggs

1 tablespoon Dijon mustard (optional)

2 1/4 cups (9 ounces) finely grated Parmesan

1 cup dried bread crumbs

1/2 teaspoon kosher salt

1/4 teaspoon black pepper

1 to 1 1/2 pounds chicken cutlets

6 tablespoons olive oil

1 head Boston or butter lettuce

1 lemon, cut into wedges

In a shallow bowl, whisk together the eggs and mustard (if using). In a separate bowl, combine 2 cups of the Parmesan, the bread crumbs, salt, and pepper. Rinse the chicken and pat it dry with paper towels. Dip one of the cutlets into the egg mixture, allowing any excess to drip off, then coat it in the bread-crumb mixture. Transfer to a plate. Repeat with the remaining chicken, batter, and bread-crumb mixture. Heat 2 tablespoons of the oil in a nonstick skillet over medium-high heat. Add half of the cutlets. Cook, turning once, until browned and cooked through, 3 to 5 minutes per side. Transfer to a plate. Carefully wipe out the skillet, add 2 more tablespoons of the oil, and re-peat with the remaining cutlets. Divide the cutlets and lettuce leaves among individual plates. Driz-zle the lettuce with the remaining oil and sprinkle with the remaining Parmesan. Serve the lemon wedges on the side.

•••Tip

If you'd rather not spend the extra money for thin cutlets, you can substitute chicken breasts as long as you flatten them to an even thinness. Place them in between 2 pieces of plastic wrap and roll or pound them using a rolling pin, a meat pounder, a heavy skillet, or even a wine bottle.

no-shop meals

PASTA WITH PEAS AND LEMON

hands-on time: 15 minutes | total time: 25 minutes | makes 4 servings

1 pound dry spaghetti or fettuccine

3 tablespoons olive oil

4 cloves garlic, thinly sliced

2 jalapeños, seeded and thinly
   sliced (optional)
   Zest of 1 lemon, grated

1/3 cup fresh lemon juice

1 1/2 cups frozen peas, thawed
   (or less, if it's all you have)

1 teaspoon kosher salt

1/8 teaspoon black pepper

1/3 cup (2 ounces) grated Parmesan
   (optional)

Cook the pasta according to the package directions. Meanwhile, heat 2 tablespoons of the oil in a large skillet over medium-low heat. Add the garlic, jalapeños (if using), and lemon zest and cook until the garlic is golden but not browned, 4 to 5 minutes. Drain the pasta and add it to the skillet with the lemon juice, peas, salt, pepper, and the remaining oil. Heat until warmed through, 3 to 4 minutes. Transfer the pasta to individual plates and sprinkle with the Parmesan (if using).

and the next time, try...
Reaching for angel-hair pasta, capellini, or vermicelli. The thinner strands cook in a fraction of the time thicker pastas take.

••• Tip
The amount of juice you can squeeze from a lemon varies significantly. Assume you'll get no less than 2 tablespoons, no more than 4.

CHEDDAR FRENCH TOAST WITH SIZZLED TOMATOES

hands-on time: 35 minutes | total time: 45 minutes | makes 4 to 8 servings

2 large eggs

1¹/₂ cups heavy cream or milk

³/₄ teaspoon kosher salt

1¹/₂ cups (6 ounces) grated sharp Cheddar

1 tablespoon fresh thyme leaves
or 1 teaspoon dried thyme (optional)

8 thick slices country-style bread

4 tablespoons unsalted butter

2 red or green tomatoes, thickly sliced

¹/₂ teaspoon black pepper

1 tablespoon olive oil

With a fork, combine the eggs, cream or milk, and ¹/₂ teaspoon of the salt in a baking dish. Add the Cheddar and thyme (if using). Soak 2 of the bread slices in the batter for 1 or 2 minutes, turning them once. Meanwhile, melt 1 tablespoon of the butter in a large nonstick skillet over medium heat. With a spatula, lift the bread from the bowl, allowing any excess batter to drip off, and transfer it to the skillet. Use a fork to transfer some of the cheese from the batter to the bread. Cook the bread until golden, 3 to 4 minutes per side. Transfer to a plate and cover to keep warm. Wipe out the skillet with a paper towel. Repeat with the remaining butter, bread, and batter. Season the tomatoes with the remaining salt and the pepper. Wipe out the skillet and return to medium heat. Heat the oil. Add the tomatoes and cook for 2 minutes per side. Serve alongside the French toast.

••• Tip

Use a loaf of sturdy, preferably day-old, country-style or Italian bread when you make French toast. Light, fluffy baguettes and sliced sandwich breads tend to become soggy.

no-shop meals

SALSA QUESADILLAS

hands-on time: 15 minutes | total time: 25 minutes | makes 4 servings

8 8-inch flour tortillas
2 cups (8 ounces) grated mozzarella
  or Monterey Jack
1 14- to 16-ounce jar store-bought
  salsa, drained
  Several leaves fresh basil or
  cilantro (optional)
4 teaspoons olive oil

Arrange 4 of the tortillas on a work surface. Divide the mozzarella, salsa, and herbs (if using) among the tortillas, leaving a 1-inch border. Top with the remaining tortillas. Heat the oil in a skillet over medium heat. Cook one quesadilla at a time, turning once, until the cheese melts and the tortillas are crisp and golden, about 2 minutes per side. Transfer to a cutting board. Repeat with the remaining quesadillas. Cut into wedges and serve.

and the next time, try...
Serving up more surprising versions of this no-fail family favorite:
• Make breakfast quesadillas with peanut butter, banana, and honey.
• Turn them into a gooey dessert with a generous smear of Nutella.
• Take advantage of Thanksgiving leftovers by layering turkey, mashed potatoes, some cheese, and a spoonful of cranberry sauce.

••• Tip
To save time, broil the quesadillas all together. Arrange them on a baking sheet, brush the tops with olive oil, and broil, turning once, until the cheese melts and the tortillas are golden brown.

SAUCY EGGS

hands-on time: 5 minutes | total time: 15 minutes | makes 2 to 4 servings

1 24- to 26-ounce jar pasta sauce
4 large eggs
1/4 teaspoon kosher salt
1/4 teaspoon black pepper (optional)
Chopped fresh basil leaves (optional)
Cooked pasta or thickly sliced bread (optional)

Bring the pasta sauce to a simmer in a large skillet over medium heat. Break one of the eggs into a small dish. Hold the dish close to the skillet and carefully tip the egg into the sauce. Repeat with the remaining eggs. If you want runny yolks, leave the tops of the eggs uncovered; if you prefer firm yolks, spoon some of the sauce over the top. Cover the skillet, reduce heat, and simmer for 10 to 12 minutes. Season with the salt and pepper (if using). Sprinkle with the basil and serve with the pasta or bread, if desired.

and the next time, try...
Fancying up this no-frills recipe:
• Sauté some garlic or onions, or both, in olive oil before adding the pasta sauce.
• Throw in some olives or capers when you add the pasta sauce.
• Sprinkle with grated Parmesan or Pecorino just before serving.

•••Tip
Consider splurging on a pricey jarred pasta sauce. When dinner consists of just 2 or 3 ingredients, each one counts.

no-shop meals

CRISPED LEFTOVER PASTA

hands-on time: 10 minutes | total time: 25 minutes | makes 1 to 2 servings

About 4 ounces cooked, unsauced
spaghetti or fettuccine, cold

2 teaspoons olive oil

3 slices prosciutto or 2 slices bacon,
(optional)

1/4 teaspoon red pepper flakes
(optional)

1/4 cup (1 ounce) grated Parmesan,
plus more for serving

1/4 teaspoon kosher salt

1/8 teaspoon black pepper

Let the pasta sit at room temperature until it be-
comes pliable, about 10 minutes. Meanwhile, heat
the oil in a nonstick skillet over medium heat. Add
the prosciutto or bacon (if using) and cook until
crisp. Transfer to a paper towel–lined plate. Drain
off and discard all but 2 teaspoons of the drippings
in the skillet. Sprinkle the red pepper flakes (if
using) over the remaining drippings. Increase heat
to medium-high. Add the pasta to the skillet and
gently spread it out to form a large nest. Cook,
without stirring, until the pasta begins to crisp and
brown on the bottom, 4 to 5 minutes. Sprinkle with
the Parmesan and prosciutto or bacon (if using).
Cook, still without stirring, for about 2 more minutes. Season with the salt and black pepper. Slide
or invert the pasta onto a plate and sprinkle with
additional Parmesan. Cut into wedges, if desired.

••• Tip

Store leftover spaghetti
on a dinner plate covered
with plastic wrap. This
creates a perfect-size
nest of noodles that you
can slide straight into
the skillet.

CHAPTER THREE

30-minute meals

Sure, Einstein devoted two whole theories to the relativity of time. But the only evidence *you* need is that your half-hour commute seems interminable—yet the 30 minutes you have to prepare dinner go by at warp speed. On those far-too-frequent evenings when you're in a race with the clock, rely on these genius recipes, all guaranteed to be on the table in a half hour or less. They may not make time slow down, but they do make every second count.

30-minute meals

STEAK WITH ROOT VEGETABLES

hands-on time: 30 minutes | total time: 30 minutes | makes 4 servings

4 8-ounce New York, strip, or sirloin
   steaks, about 1 inch thick
2 teaspoons kosher salt
1/2 teaspoon black pepper
3 tablespoons olive oil
2 carrots, cut lengthwise into
   thin strips
2 parsnips, cut lengthwise into
   thin strips
2 beets, cut into thin slices
1 tablespoon chopped fresh tarragon

Season the steaks with 1 1/2 teaspoons of the salt and 1/4 teaspoon of the pepper. Heat 1 tablespoon of the oil in a large skillet over medium-high heat. Add some of the steaks to the skillet and cook to the desired doneness, about 4 minutes per side for medium-rare. Transfer to a plate and cover loosely with foil. Repeat with the remaining steaks. Let rest. Meanwhile, wipe out the skillet with paper towels. Heat the remaining oil over medium-low heat. Add the carrots, parsnips, and beets and cook until tender, 5 to 7 minutes. Season with the remaining salt and pepper and the tarragon. Serve the vegetables alongside the steaks.

and the next time, try...
Substituting any root vegetable for the carrots, parsnips, or beets. Rutabagas and sweet potatoes work particularly well.

••• Tip
To shave a few minutes off this recipe, slice the carrots and parsnips horizontally into thin coins rather than lengthwise into thin strips.

30-minute meals

LINGUINE WITH ARTICHOKES AND LEEKS

hands-on time: 25 minutes | total time: 30 minutes | makes 4 servings

1 pound dry linguine or fettuccine
2 medium leeks (white and light green
  parts only), rinsed
2 12-ounce jars artichoke hearts
  (packed in oil), drained
3 tablespoons olive oil
1 tablespoon fresh lemon juice
3 teaspoons kosher salt
1 teaspoon black pepper
1/2 cup (2 ounces) grated Parmesan

Cook the pasta according to the package directions. Meanwhile, halve the leeks lengthwise and thickly slice them crosswise. Halve the artichokes lengthwise. Heat the oil in a large skillet over medium-low heat. Add the leeks and cook, stirring frequently, until softened but not browned, about 5 minutes. Transfer to a plate; set aside. Increase heat to medium and add the artichokes. Cook for 3 minutes per side. Add the leeks, lemon juice, salt, and pepper and toss. Transfer to a large bowl. Drain the pasta. Add it and 1/4 cup of the Parmesan to the vegetables and toss. Serve with the remaining Parmesan on the side.

••• Tip

Leeks tend to trap quite a lot of sand between their layers. To get rid of the grit, halve them, place them in a large bowl of cold water, and swirl. Then wait for a minute. After the dirt settles, lift the leeks out.

GRILLED SHRIMP TACOS

hands-on time: 30 minutes | total time: 30 minutes | makes 4 servings

1/2 cup sour cream

3 tablespoons mayonnaise

3 tablespoons milk

1/2 teaspoon ground cumin

3 tablespoons unsalted butter, melted

2 cloves garlic, finely chopped

11/2 pounds large shrimp, peeled and deveined

4 limes, quartered

1/2 teaspoon kosher salt

8 6-inch corn tortillas

3 cups shredded green cabbage

1 14- to 16-ounce jar green (tomatillo) salsa

Wooden skewers, soaked in water for at least 30 minutes

In a small bowl, whisk together the sour cream, mayonnaise, milk, and cumin; set aside. In a separate bowl, combine the butter and garlic. Heat a grill or broiler. Rinse the shrimp and pat them dry with paper towels. Place the shrimp and lime wedges on the skewers. Brush the shrimp with the garlic butter. Grill or broil until the shrimp are cooked through and the limes are browned, about 3 minutes per side. Season the shrimp with the salt. Transfer to a plate. Grill or broil the tortillas until warmed, about 30 seconds per side. Place them between clean towels to keep warm. To serve, remove the shrimp from the skewers, divide them evenly among the tortillas, and top each with the cabbage, sour cream mixture, and salsa. Serve the lime wedges on the side.

•••Tip

Skewer your shrimp twice—that way, they'll lie flat on the grill and won't spin when you turn them. First spear the shrimp through the tail, then bend the shrimp and spear it through the head.

30-minute meals

GRILLED TUNA WITH TOMATO SALSA

hands-on time: 15 minutes | total time: 25 minutes | makes 4 servings

Zest of 1 lemon, grated

3 tablespoons fresh lemon juice

1 teaspoon honey

1 small shallot, finely chopped

1 clove garlic, finely chopped

1 tablespoon fresh oregano
or 2 teaspoons dried oregano

1/2 cup extra-virgin olive oil

1/2 teaspoon kosher salt

1/4 teaspoon black pepper

4 6- to 8-ounce tuna steaks

2 tomatoes, seeded (if desired)
and diced

2 tablespoons capers,
roughly chopped

1 cup arugula, roughly chopped

In a medium bowl, whisk together the lemon zest and juice, honey, shallot, garlic, and oregano. Whisking constantly, slowly add the oil in a steady stream. Season with the salt and pepper. Rinse the tuna steaks and pat them dry with paper towels. Arrange them in a baking dish and drizzle with 1/2 cup of the lemon mixture. Turn to coat. Heat a grill or grill pan on high. Transfer the tuna to the grill or pan. Cook to the desired doneness, about 4 minutes per side for medium-rare. Meanwhile, to make the tomato salsa, add the tomatoes, capers, and arugula to the remaining lemon mixture and toss. Serve the salsa with the tuna.

and the next time, try...
Drizzling the lemon mixture over cooked chicken cutlets or pork chops. It's a faster—and even more flavorful—alternative to marinating.

···•Tip
To seed a tomato, cut it in half crosswise and grasp half in your hand, cut-side down. Hold it over a sink and flick your wrist sharply several times. The seeds should fly right out.

CHICKEN CUTLETS WITH HERB SAUCE

hands-on time: 10 minutes | total time: 30 minutes | makes 4 servings

1 tablespoon olive oil

1 1/2 pounds Yukon gold or new potatoes, cut into 1/2-inch pieces (peel first, if desired)

1 1/2 teaspoons kosher salt

1 to 1 1/2 pounds chicken cutlets

1/4 teaspoon black pepper

1/4 cup dry white wine

2 tablespoons unsalted butter, chilled

2 tablespoons chopped fresh herbs, such as rosemary, chives, parsley, or tarragon

Heat oven to 425° F. Heat the oil in a large skillet over medium-high heat. Add the potatoes and cook, stirring occasionally, until golden, about 15 minutes. Transfer to a baking dish and season with 1 teaspoon of the salt. Bake for 10 minutes. Meanwhile, rinse the chicken and pat it dry with paper towels. Season on both sides with 1/4 teaspoon of the salt and 1/8 teaspoon of the pepper. Return the skillet to medium-high heat. Add the chicken and cook until browned on each side and cooked through, 3 to 4 minutes per side. Transfer the chicken to a platter. Add the wine to the skillet, reduce heat, and simmer for 2 minutes, constantly stirring and scraping the bottom. Add 1 tablespoon of the butter and stir or whisk until completely combined. Repeat with the remaining butter. Remove the skillet from heat. Add the herbs and the remaining salt and pepper and whisk to combine. Add the potatoes to the platter with the chicken and spoon the sauce over the top.

••• Tip

Want the secret to a smooth, silky sauce? Use cold butter and slowly whisk it into the pan sauce. If you use room-temperature butter, it won't emulsify as nicely.

30-minute meals

PORK CHOPS WITH LEMONY BREAD CRUMBS

hands-on time: 20 minutes | total time: 30 minutes | makes 4 servings

   3 tablespoons extra-virgin olive oil
   8 thin-cut pork chops
   3 teaspoons kosher salt
 1/2 teaspoon black pepper
   1 14- to 16-ounce jar pasta sauce
 1/2 cup dry bread crumbs
   2 tablespoons chopped fresh sage
     Zest of 1 lemon, grated
   1 clove garlic, crushed
 1/2 pound green beans
 1 1/2 cups arugula
   1 tablespoon fresh lemon juice

Heat oven to 350° F. Heat 1 tablespoon of the oil in a large ovenproof skillet over medium-high heat. Season the pork with 1/2 teaspoon of the salt and 1/4 teaspoon of the pepper. Cook until browned but not cooked through, about 2 minutes per side. Remove skillet from heat. Spoon the pasta sauce over the pork. In a small bowl, combine the bread crumbs, sage, lemon zest, garlic, 1/2 teaspoon of the salt, and the remaining pepper. Sprinkle the bread-crumb mixture evenly over the sauce. Transfer the skillet to oven and roast until the sauce is bubbling, about 10 minutes. Meanwhile, bring a large pot of water and the remaining salt to a boil. Add the beans, return to a boil, and cook until tender, 3 to 5 minutes. Drain and transfer to a bowl of ice water. Drain again and return to the bowl. Add the arugula, lemon juice, and the remaining oil and toss. Serve the salad alongside the pork.

••• Tip

You can use plain canned tomato sauce in place of the jarred pasta sauce if that's all you have in your cupboard. It will just make a slightly less rich sauce.

30-minute meals

CHICKEN SOUVLAKI

hands-on time: 25 minutes | total time: 30 minutes | makes 4 servings

4 pieces flat bread or pitas

2¹/₂ teaspoons red wine vinegar

1 tablespoon fresh lemon juice

1¹/₂ tablespoons fresh oregano
or 1¹/₂ teaspoons dried oregano

1¹/₂ tablespoons fresh thyme
or 1¹/₂ teaspoons dried thyme

¹/₄ teaspoon black pepper

¹/₄ cup extra-virgin olive oil

2 medium tomatoes, cut
into wedges

¹/₂ small red onion, thinly sliced

³/₄ cup (3 ounces) crumbled Feta

¹/₄ cup kalamata olives, pitted
if desired

4 boneless, skinless chicken breast
halves, cut into 4-inch pieces

¹/₂ cup plain yogurt

1 small cucumber, roughly chopped
(peel first, if desired)

1¹/₂ tablespoons finely chopped
fresh dill

Heat oven to 250° F. Wrap the bread in foil and place in oven to warm. Meanwhile, in a large bowl, combine 1¹/₂ teaspoons of the vinegar, the lemon juice, oregano, thyme, and pepper. Whisking constantly, slowly add the oil in a steady stream. In a separate bowl, combine the tomatoes, onion, Feta, and olives. Pour 2¹/₂ tablespoons of the vinaigrette over the tomato mixture and toss; set aside. Rinse the chicken and pat it dry with paper towels. Add it to the remaining vinaigrette and toss. Heat a grill or broiler on high. Cook the chicken, turning occasionally, until cooked through, 5 to 7 minutes total. Meanwhile, combine the yogurt, cucumber, dill, and the remaining vinegar in a bowl. Spoon some of the cucumber mixture onto each piece of bread and top with the chicken and the tomato salad.

and the next time, try...
Preparing the souvlaki the traditional way—with lamb. You can also use turkey or shrimp.

••• Tip

For an extra-thick and creamy spread, drain the yogurt to remove excess liquid. Place a paper towel–lined strainer over a bowl, spoon in the yogurt, then refrigerate for at least 20 minutes.

30-minute meals

SOY-GLAZED SALMON WITH NOODLES

hands-on time: 30 minutes | total time: 30 minutes | makes 4 servings

1/2 pound green beans, sliced in
    half lengthwise

1 pound soba noodles or
    whole-wheat spaghetti

1/2 cup plus 3 tablespoons low-sodium
    soy sauce

1 clove garlic, finely chopped

1 tablespoon finely grated
    ginger, plus 2 tablespoons thinly
    sliced ginger

2 tablespoons rice wine, sherry,
    or white wine

4 6-ounce salmon fillets,
    skin removed

3 scallions, cut into 2-inch pieces

1/4 cup rice vinegar

2 tablespoons fresh lemon juice

1 tablespoon granulated sugar

Heat oven to 400° F. Bring a large pot of water to a boil. Add the beans and cook until tender, about 2 minutes. Using a slotted spoon, transfer the beans to a bowl of ice water. Drain and set aside. Add the noodles to the boiling water and cook according to the package directions. Meanwhile, in a baking dish, combine 3 tablespoons of the soy sauce, the garlic, grated ginger, and 1 tablespoon of the wine. Rinse the salmon and pat it dry with paper towels. Add it to the baking dish and turn to coat. Scatter the sliced ginger and scallions over the top. Cover with foil and bake until the fish is the same color throughout and flakes easily, about 20 minutes. Meanwhile, in a small saucepan, combine the vinegar, lemon juice, sugar, and the remaining soy sauce and wine, stirring until the sugar dissolves. Bring to a boil and cook until reduced by half, about 3 minutes. Remove from heat and cover to keep warm. Divide the drained noodles and beans among individual plates, top each with a salmon fillet, and drizzle with the glaze.

••• Tip

If you ask nicely, most fishmongers will remove the skin from a fish fillet for you. If you forget—or yours refuses—grab hold of one edge of the fish, place a knife between the skin and the flesh, and run the blade along the length of the fillet. To prevent your fingers from slipping, grasp the fish through a paper towel.

SOY-MARINATED LONDON BROIL

hands-on time: 15 minutes | total time: 25 minutes | makes 4 servings

½ cup low-sodium soy sauce

¼ cup light brown sugar,
   firmly packed

1 clove garlic, thinly sliced

1½ pounds top round London broil,
   about 1½ inches thick

½ teaspoon black pepper

8 scallions, trimmed
   Cooked white rice

1 tablespoon sesame seeds

In a large saucepan, off the heat, combine the soy sauce, brown sugar, and garlic, stirring until the sugar dissolves. Rinse the meat and pat it dry with paper towels. Add the meat to the marinade and turn to coat. (If you have the time, you can cover the saucepan and refrigerate it for at least 30 minutes and up to 8 hours for a more intense soy flavor.) Heat broiler. Transfer the meat to a rimmed baking sheet lined with foil, reserving the marinade in the saucepan. Sprinkle the meat with the pepper. Broil to the desired doneness, about 5 minutes per side for medium-rare. Transfer to a cutting board and let rest for 5 minutes. Meanwhile, place the saucepan containing the marinade over medium-high heat and bring to a boil. Add the scallions, reduce heat, and simmer for 2 minutes. Thinly slice the meat across the grain. To serve, divide the rice among individual bowls and arrange the meat on top. Spoon the scallions and sauce over the meat, and sprinkle with the sesame seeds.

••• Tip

Slice the meat at a slant across the grain to ensure maximum tenderness. This technique works on most relatively inexpensive cuts of steak, including flank, skirt, and top round.

30-minute meals

NOT-SO-SLOPPY JOES

hands-on time: 20 minutes | total time: 30 minutes | makes 4 servings

1 tablespoon olive oil
1 small yellow onion, finely chopped
1 clove garlic, finely chopped
1 red bell pepper, finely chopped
1 pound ground beef
1 6-ounce can tomato paste
1½ teaspoons chili powder
1 teaspoon ground cumin
⅛ teaspoon black pepper
⅛ teaspoon ground cinnamon
1 teaspoon kosher salt
4 hamburger buns, toasted
½ cup (2 ounces) grated Cheddar (optional)
½ cup sour cream (optional)

Heat the oil in a large saucepan over medium heat. Add the onion, garlic, and bell pepper. Cook until softened, about 3 minutes. Add the beef and cook, crumbling it with a spoon, until no trace of pink remains, about 7 minutes. Spoon off and discard any excess fat. Stir in the tomato paste, chili powder, cumin, black pepper, cinnamon, and salt. Simmer, stirring occasionally, until the sauce thickens slightly, about 12 minutes. Spoon the beef mixture onto the bottom half of each bun and top with the Cheddar and a dollop of the sour cream (if using). Sandwich with the top half of each bun.

and the next time, try...
Trading in the beef for ground turkey or even vegetarian meat crumbles. Given the sauce's piquant flavor, no one will ever taste the difference.

•••Tip
Don't forget to toast the buns. This quick but necessary step ensures that the bread doesn't turn to mush the second the juices hit the roll.

30-minute meals

SAUSAGES WITH WARM TOMATOES AND HASH BROWNS

hands-on time: 30 minutes | total time: 30 minutes | makes 4 servings

2 tablespoons olive oil

8 sweet Italian sausage links

4 tablespoons unsalted butter

1 1/2 pounds russet potatoes, peeled and grated

1 small yellow onion, grated

2 teaspoons kosher salt

1 teaspoon black pepper

1/4 cup plus 2 tablespoons chopped fresh flat-leaf parsley leaves

18 cherry or grape tomatoes (red, yellow, or orange), halved

Heat the oil in a large skillet over medium heat. Prick the sausages with a fork. Cook, turning occasionally, until browned and cooked through, about 20 minutes. Meanwhile, melt the butter in another large skillet over medium heat. Add the potatoes and onion and cook until softened, about 5 minutes. Season with 1 1/2 teaspoons of the salt, 1/2 teaspoon of the pepper, and 1/4 cup of the parsley. Gently press the potatoes into the bottom of the skillet with a spatula. Cook, without stirring, until a crust forms, about 5 minutes. Then use the spatula to break apart the potatoes, turn the pieces, and press down again. Cook until another crust forms, about 5 minutes. Cover, reduce heat to medium-low, and cook for 10 minutes. Meanwhile, transfer the sausages to a plate and cover with foil to keep warm. Spoon off and discard all but about 2 tablespoons of the fat from the skillet that contained the sausages. Add the tomatoes and the remaining salt, pepper, and parsley. Cook until the tomatoes soften slightly, about 5 minutes. Serve the sausages with the hash browns and tomatoes.

••• Tip

For faster cooking, halve the sausage links lengthwise before adding them to the skillet. (You can also try this speedy technique with hot dogs.)

30-minute meals

POACHED HALIBUT WITH GREEN BEANS AND RED POTATOES

hands-on time: 25 minutes | total time: 30 minutes | makes 4 servings

1 pound red potatoes

2½ teaspoons kosher salt

1 pound green beans

4 6-ounce halibut fillets,
skin removed

¼ teaspoon black pepper

About 2½ cups dry white wine

3 tablespoons unsalted butter

2 tablespoons chopped fresh chives

Place the potatoes and 2 teaspoons of the salt in a large pot. Add enough cold water to cover. Bring to a boil. Reduce heat and simmer until the potatoes are almost fork-tender, 15 to 20 minutes. Add the green beans and cook until both the potatoes and the beans are tender, 5 minutes more. Meanwhile, rinse the halibut fillets and pat them dry with paper towels. Season with ¼ teaspoon of the remaining salt and ⅛ teaspoon of the pepper. Place the fillets in a large skillet and add just enough wine to reach halfway up the sides of the fillets. Bring to a simmer over medium-low heat. Cover and cook until the fillets are the same color throughout and flake easily, 6 to 8 minutes. Transfer to individual plates. Drain the potatoes and beans. Quarter the potatoes. Divide the potatoes and beans among the plates. Return the pot to medium-low heat. Add the butter, chives, and the remaining salt and pepper and heat until the butter melts. Drizzle the butter mixture over the halibut, potatoes, and beans.

••• Tip

When you chop fresh herbs—whether it's chives, basil, parsley, mint, tarragon, or cilantro—reach for the scissors rather than a knife. They make quick work of the task and keep the leaves from bruising (which can cause them to turn an unappetizing shade of black).

30-minute meals

PASTA WITH BROCCOLI RABE AND SAUSAGE

hands-on time: 20 minutes | total time: 30 minutes | makes 4 servings

1 pound dry rigatoni, penne, or ziti

1 tablespoon olive oil

1 pound chicken or pork sausage, casings removed

2 cloves garlic, thinly sliced

1 14.5-ounce can low-sodium chicken broth

1/8 teaspoon red pepper flakes

1 bunch broccoli rabe, trimmed and cut into 1-inch pieces

4 tablespoons unsalted butter

1 1/2 cups (6 ounces) grated Parmesan

1/4 teaspoon kosher salt

1/4 teaspoon black pepper

Cook the pasta according to the package directions. Meanwhile, heat the oil in a large saucepan over medium heat. Add the sausage and cook, crumbling it with a spoon, until no trace of pink remains, about 7 minutes. Spoon off and discard any excess fat. Add the garlic and cook for 1 minute. Add the broth and red pepper flakes and bring to a boil. Add the broccoli rabe, cover, and cook until tender, about 3 minutes. Stir in the butter and Parmesan and cook, uncovered, until the sauce thickens slightly, about 2 minutes. Add the drained pasta, salt, and black pepper and toss to combine. Set aside for a few minutes before serving to allow the pasta to absorb some of the flavorful liquid. To serve, divide the pasta among individual bowls.

and the next time, try...
Using a less pungent green in place of the broccoli rabe. Try broccoli florets to create a milder version or, for a more peppery dish, go with Swiss chard.

••• Tip

Cook pasta in plenty of salted water. The salt will help bring out the natural flavor of the pasta, and the generous amount of water will prevent the noodles from sticking to one another.

30-minute meals

SPICED LAMB CHOPS WITH CHICKPEA SALAD

hands-on time: 20 minutes | total time: 30 minutes | makes 4 servings

1 15-ounce can chickpeas,
   drained and rinsed
4 plum tomatoes, thickly sliced
1 small yellow or red onion,
   sliced into half-moons
3/4 cup fresh flat-leaf parsley leaves,
   roughly chopped
3/4 cup fresh mint leaves, chopped
2 teaspoons white wine vinegar
1 clove garlic, crushed
5 tablespoons olive oil
   Zest of 1 lemon, grated
3 tablespoons fresh lemon juice
1 teaspoon kosher salt
1/2 teaspoon black pepper
1 tablespoon ground cumin
1 tablespoon ground coriander
1 teaspoon paprika
8 lamb loin chops

In a large bowl, combine the chickpeas, tomatoes, onion, parsley, mint, vinegar, garlic, 3 tablespoons of the oil, the lemon zest and juice, 1/2 teaspoon of the salt, and 1/4 teaspoon of the pepper; set aside. In a separate bowl, combine the cumin, coriander, paprika, and the remaining salt and pepper. Lightly coat each of the lamb chops with the spice mixture. Heat 1 tablespoon of the remaining oil in a skillet over medium-high heat. Add half of the lamb chops to the skillet, being careful not to crowd them. Cook to the desired doneness, 2 to 3 minutes per side for medium-rare. Transfer to a plate. Repeat with the remaining oil and lamb chops. Divide the chickpea salad among individual plates and top each salad with 2 lamb chops.

and the next time, try...
Making the salad with canned, drained white beans instead of chickpeas.

••• Tip
Lamb loin chops are exceptionally tender, reasonably priced cuts. Do not confuse them with rib chops, which are daintier and more expensive.

LEMON-HERB SEAFOOD STIR-FRY

hands-on time: 30 minutes | total time: 30 minutes | makes 4 servings

1/4 cup low-sodium soy sauce

2 1/2 tablespoons fresh lemon juice

2 large cloves garlic, finely chopped

1 1/2 tablespoons sugar

1 1/2 tablespoons chopped fresh
   basil leaves

1 1/2 tablespoons chopped fresh
   cilantro leaves

1 pound sea scallops

2 1/2 tablespoons olive oil

1/3 pound sugar snap peas

5 ounces fresh spinach
   or watercress
   Cooked white rice, preferably
   jasmine or basmati

In a small bowl, combine the soy sauce, lemon juice, garlic, and sugar, stirring until the sugar dissolves. Add the basil and cilantro; set aside. Rinse the scallops and pat them dry with paper towels. Heat a wok or large skillet over medium-high heat. Add 2 tablespoons of the oil and heat for 30 seconds. Add the scallops. Cook on one side until browned, about 3 minutes. Turn and cook until the scallops are the same color throughout, 1 to 2 minutes more. Transfer to a plate. Wipe out the pan with a paper towel. Add the remaining oil and heat for 30 seconds. Add the peas and 2 tablespoons of water. Cover partially and cook, stirring occasionally, until the peas are bright green, about 1 minute. Add the spinach or watercress and the lemon-herb sauce. When the sauce starts bubbling, add the scallops. Stir-fry until warmed through, about 1 minute. Serve over the rice.

••• **Tip**

As you heat the oil, keep an eye on the wok. If you see wisps of smoke rising from the pan— a telltale sign the temperature is too high—carefully pour out the oil, wipe out the pan with a paper towel, and start over.

CHAPTER FOUR

no-cook meals

Whether you blame it on an oppressive summer heat wave or on your oppressive work schedule, there are some nights when you simply cannot bear to turn on the stove. But a night without cooking doesn't have to mean a night with takeout. Instead, try your hand at cutting-board cuisine—a far more interesting (and often healthier) alternative. With just a few fresh ingredients, a knife, and—you guessed it—a cutting board, you'll be ready to serve supper without going anywhere near a burner...or a drive-thru.

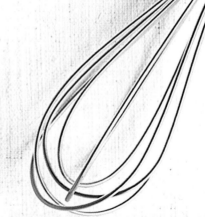

CANTALOUPE SOUP WITH PROSCIUTTO AND MOZZARELLA SANDWICHES

hands-on time: 25 minutes | total time: 25 minutes | makes 6 to 8 servings

2 baguettes

2 8-ounce balls fresh mozzarella, thickly sliced

1/2 pound prosciutto, thinly sliced

2 tablespoons extra-virgin olive oil

1/4 teaspoon black pepper

2 cantaloupes, chilled

1/2 teaspoon kosher salt

16 fresh mint leaves, chopped if desired

Halve each baguette lengthwise, then cut it crosswise into 3 or 4 portions. Place some of the mozzarella and prosciutto on the bottom half of each portion. Drizzle with the oil and sprinkle with the pepper. Sandwich with the top half of each baguette portion. Transfer to individual plates. Halve each cantaloupe and remove and discard the seeds. Scoop the melon into a blender. Add the salt and puree until smooth. Pour into individual bowls and sprinkle with the mint. Serve alongside the prosciutto and mozzarella sandwiches.

•••Tip

To select a ripe cantaloupe, look beneath the raised pattern on the melon's rind. The background color should be cream, not green. If you're still uncertain, smell it close to the stem end; it should have a sweet, faintly musty aroma. The ends should also yield slightly to pressure.

no-cook meals

CHICKEN SALAD WITH PEACHES AND BLUE CHEESE

hands-on time: 20 minutes | total time: 20 minutes | makes 6 servings

2　heads romaine lettuce, leaves cut crosswise into 1-inch strips

1　store-bought rotisserie chicken, meat sliced into bite-size pieces

2　peaches, roughly chopped (peel first, if desired)

3/4　cup (3 ounces) crumbled blue cheese

1/2　cup (2 ounces) almonds, roughly chopped

1/4　cup white wine vinegar

1/4　cup extra-virgin olive oil

1　teaspoon kosher salt

1/4　teaspoon black pepper

Arrange the lettuce, chicken, peaches, cheese, and almonds on a platter or on individual plates. Whisk together the vinegar, oil, salt, and pepper in a small bowl. Drizzle the vinaigrette over the salad.

and the next time, try...
Customizing the salad based on the season—or the contents of your refrigerator:
• Use thinly sliced pears or halved red grapes in place of the peaches.
• Replace the romaine lettuce with spinach, arugula, or watercress.
• Swap goat cheese for the blue.
• Go with walnuts instead of the almonds.

•••Tip
The best blue cheeses for salads are dry and crumbly in texture and not overwhelmingly pungent. Try a Roquefort or a Maytag blue.

SMOKED SALMON WITH CUCUMBER AND WATERCRESS

hands-on time: 15 minutes | total time: 20 minutes | makes 6 servings

2 bunches watercress, ends trimmed

1 pound smoked salmon, thinly sliced

4 teaspoons prepared horseradish

4 teaspoons coarse-grain mustard

1/2 cup sour cream

1/4 cup fresh lemon juice

1/2 teaspoon kosher salt

1/4 teaspoon black pepper

2 small cucumbers

Bagel chips, crackers, or thinly sliced baguette, toasted

Separate the watercress into single sprigs. Arrange the watercress and salmon on a platter or on individual plates. In a bowl, whisk together the horseradish, mustard, sour cream, lemon juice, salt, and pepper until smooth. Transfer half the dressing to a small serving bowl; set aside. Halve each cucumber lengthwise and thinly slice. Add the cucumbers to the remaining dressing and toss to coat. Divide the cucumber mixture among the plates. Serve with the bagel chips, crackers, or toasted bread and the reserved dressing.

••• Tip

Seeding a cucumber that is destined for a salad isn't required, but it will make the salad less watery. Just halve the cucumber lengthwise, then use a spoon to scoop out and discard the seeds.

no-cook meals

SWEET PEA AND MINT SOUP

hands-on time: 15 minutes | total time: 15 minutes | makes 4 servings

2 10-ounce packages (4 cups) frozen
  peas, thawed slightly

¾ cup fresh mint leaves

4 scallions, roughly chopped

3 cups low-sodium chicken
  or vegetable broth

1 teaspoon kosher salt

1 teaspoon sugar

Place all the ingredients in a blender. Puree until smooth, at least 1 minute. To serve, pour into individual bowls.

and the next time, try...
Embellishing this delicate recipe with a few simple touches:
• Strain the soup for a silky smooth texture.
• Add a dollop of crème fraîche, sour cream, or plain yogurt.
• Sprinkle with torn fresh mint leaves.

••• Tip
Keep a few bags of frozen peas around at all times. Not only do the peas retain a surprisingly fresh, springlike flavor when frozen but the bags make great impromptu ice packs.

TUNA IN A TOMATO

hands-on time: 20 minutes | total time: 20 minutes | makes 6 servings

6 large tomatoes

3 6-ounce cans tuna, drained

3 tablespoons capers, roughly chopped

1 cup fresh flat-leaf parsley leaves, roughly chopped

Zest of 1 lemon

1/4 cup fresh lemon juice

1 tablespoon extra-virgin olive oil

1/4 teaspoon black pepper

With a paring knife, cut out and discard the stem of each tomato. Using a spoon, hollow out the tomatoes, leaving each with a 1/4-inch shell, and transfer the pulp to a medium bowl. Add the remaining ingredients to the tomato pulp and toss gently. Spoon the mixture back into the tomatoes and serve.

and the next time, try...
Introducing new flavors and textures to the filling:
• Use basil in place of parsley.
• Substitute chopped olives for capers.
• Add finely chopped red onion or scallions.
• Opt for equal amounts of mayonnaise and sour cream in place of the olive oil.
• Stir in a couple of spoonfuls of cooked rice.

•••Tip

In the summer, make this recipe with heirloom tomatoes, which come in vibrant colors. Yellow and orange heirlooms tend to be less acidic than red ones; purple heirlooms are often earthier and more intense in flavor.

no-cook meals

GREEK SALAD

hands-on time: 15 minutes | total time: 15 minutes | makes 4 to 6 servings

8 tablespoons extra-virgin olive oil

1 cup fresh basil leaves

1/4 teaspoon kosher salt

8 ounces Feta, thickly sliced

1 medium cucumber, chopped
(peel first, if desired)

8 ounces cherry or grape
tomatoes, halved

3/4 cup kalamata olives, pitted
if desired

1 12-ounce jar pepperoncini, drained

2 14-ounce jars dolmades (optional)

1/4 teaspoon black pepper

1 lemon, cut into wedges

In a blender or food processor, puree the oil, basil, and salt; set aside. Arrange the Feta, cucumber, tomatoes, olives, pepperoncini, and dolmades (if using) on a platter or on individual plates. Drizzle with the basil oil and sprinkle with the pepper. Serve with the lemon wedges on the side.

and the next time, try...
Breathing new life into the leftovers by chopping them and tossing with day-old bread or freshly cooked pasta. Sprinkle with basil leaves, if you have any extra lying around.

••• Tip

Dolmades—essentially grape leaves stuffed with rice—can be found at many Greek and Italian delis, as well as in the olive aisle in supermarkets. Pepperoncini (mildly hot pickled peppers) are available in Italian delis or near the pickles in some supermarkets.

PAN BAGNAT

hands-on time: 20 minutes | total time: 20 minutes | makes 3 to 4 servings

1 baguette
2 6-ounce cans tuna, drained
1/2 teaspoon kosher salt
1/4 teaspoon black pepper
2 tablespoons fresh lemon juice
3 tablespoons extra-virgin olive oil
1 head green leaf or Boston lettuce
2 plum tomatoes, sliced crosswise
1/2 small red onion, thinly sliced
1/3 cup kalamata olives,
   pitted and roughly chopped
1/3 cup fresh basil leaves
3 tablespoons capers, roughly
   chopped (optional)

Halve the baguette lengthwise, then cut it crosswise into 3 or 4 portions. Remove some of the light, fluffy bread from the center and discard or reserve for another use (such as bread crumbs). In a medium bowl, combine the tuna, salt, pepper, lemon juice, and 1 tablespoon of the oil. Place a few lettuce leaves on both halves of each baguette portion. Top the bottom halves with the tuna mixture, tomatoes, onion, olives, basil, and capers (if using). Drizzle with the remaining oil. Sandwich with the top half of each baguette portion and press gently but firmly.

and the next time, try...
Giving this French sandwich an international flavor by replacing the baguette with whole-grain bread, pita, or whatever happens to be sitting on the counter (pumpernickel, anyone?).

•••Tip
Pit the olives by placing them on a cutting board and pressing on them with the flat side of a chef's knife. The pits should pop right out; if they're being stubborn, pinch each olive to coax the pit out.

no-cook meals

PANZANELLA

hands-on time: 25 minutes | total time: 25 minutes | makes 8 servings

1 loaf day-old whole-wheat or white bread, preferably unsliced

6 large tomatoes, cut into wedges

1 large red onion, thinly sliced

1/4 cup kalamata olives, pitted and roughly chopped if desired

1/2 cup fresh basil leaves, chopped

1/2 cup extra-virgin olive oil

1/4 cup red wine vinegar

1/4 cup fresh lemon juice

1/2 teaspoon kosher salt

1/4 cup chopped fresh flat-leaf parsley leaves (optional)

1/2 cup (2 ounces) shaved Parmesan

Remove and discard the crust from the bread, if desired. Tear or cut the bread into 1-inch pieces; you will need about 5 cups total. Place the bread in a large bowl along with the tomatoes, onion, olives, and basil. In a separate bowl, whisk together the oil, vinegar, lemon juice, salt, and parsley (if using). Drizzle the vinaigrette over the bread mixture and toss. To serve, transfer to individual plates and scatter the Parmesan over the top.

and the next time, try...
Preparing panzanella the truly Italian—if slightly soggy—way. Set it aside at room temperature for about an hour before serving to allow the bread to absorb the flavorful tomato juices and vinaigrette.

···•Tip
To shave Parmesan, pull a vegetable peeler lightly but firmly across the surface of the cheese. It will fall away in ribbons.

GAZPACHO

hands-on time: 30 minutes | total time: 2 hours, 30 minutes (includes chilling) | makes 8 servings

3 small fennel bulbs, roughly chopped

4 celery stalks, roughly chopped

1 bunch scallions, roughly chopped

1 medium sweet onion, roughly chopped

2 small cloves garlic, chopped

3 red bell peppers, roughly chopped

2 large tomatoes, diced, or one 14.5-ounce can diced tomatoes, undrained

1/2 cup extra-virgin olive oil

1 tablespoon kosher salt

1/2 teaspoon black pepper

1 32-ounce container (4 cups) tomato or vegetable juice

1/3 cup fresh lemon juice

Celery leaves (optional)

Fresh dill (optional)

Place the fennel, celery stalks, scallions, onion, garlic, and bell peppers in the bowl of a food processor. Pulse until the mixture is finely chopped and combined but not pureed. Pour the mixture into a large glass or plastic bowl. Stir in the tomatoes with their juices, oil, salt, black pepper, tomato or vegetable juice, and lemon juice. Cover and refrigerate for at least 2 hours. To serve, sprinkle with the celery leaves, dill, or both (if using).

and the next time, try...

Personalizing the recipe:

• Puree the soup for a smoother texture.

• For a touch of heat, stir in 1 teaspoon hot sauce.

• Trade in the celery leaves or dill for fresh basil.

•••Tip

Because the vegetables are destined for the food processor, there's no need to spend time dicing them precisely. Just give them a quick, rough chop.

no-cook meals

SHRIMP, WATERMELON, AND AVOCADO SALAD

hands-on time: 20 minutes | total time: 30 minutes | makes 6 servings

1 1-pound package frozen cooked shrimp, thawed

4 cups watermelon, seeded and roughly chopped

1 medium red onion, thinly sliced

1/2 cup fresh cilantro leaves

2 jalapeños, seeded and finely chopped

2 avocados, roughly chopped

Juice of 1 lime

1 teaspoon honey

3 tablespoons extra-virgin olive oil

3/4 teaspoon kosher salt

1/4 teaspoon black pepper

Place the shrimp, watermelon, onion, cilantro, jalapeños, and avocados in a large bowl. In a separate bowl, whisk together the lime juice, honey, oil, salt, and pepper. Pour the vinaigrette over the salad and toss gently. Set aside for 10 minutes before serving to allow the flavors to meld.

and the next time, try...
Tossing together a winterized version of this kaleidoscopic summery salad. Swap in sections of pink grapefruit for the watermelon cubes, and try mint in place of the cilantro.

···•Tip
Cut down on prep time (not to mention refrigerator-shelf space) by using a "personal-size" watermelon (available in most supermarkets). It weighs only 4 to 6 pounds and contains few, if any, seeds.

CHAPTER FIVE

freezer meals

The humble frozen dinner holds an esteemed position in the harried cook's kitchen. It's no mystery why: When you have to work late but your kids have to eat early, your best—some might say *only*—option is to rely on a heat-and-serve meal. To that end, the freezer-friendly recipes here are custom-designed for you to make ahead of time and use whenever. So your family can sit down to a dinner that's stick-a-fork-in-it done—whether or not you're there to join them. Talk about frozen assets.

PASTA WITH BOLOGNESE SAUCE

hands-on time: 20 minutes | total time: 1 hour, 25 minutes | makes 4 to 6 servings

1 tablespoon olive oil

1 large yellow onion, finely chopped

3 celery stalks, finely chopped

1 carrot, finely chopped

4 cloves garlic, finely chopped

1/4 pound pancetta, finely chopped

1 1/2 pounds ground beef

1 cup dry white wine

1 cup whole milk

1 6-ounce can tomato paste

1 14.5-ounce can diced tomatoes, undrained

1/4 teaspoon red pepper flakes

2 tablespoons chopped fresh oregano or 1 1/2 teaspoons dried oregano

1/2 cup fresh flat-leaf parsley leaves, chopped

2 1/2 teaspoons kosher salt

1/4 teaspoon black pepper

1/8 teaspoon grated nutmeg

1 pound dry fettuccine

Grated Parmesan

Heat the oil in a Dutch oven or large saucepan over medium heat. Add the onion and cook for 3 minutes. Add the celery, carrot, and garlic and cook for 5 minutes. Add the pancetta and cook for 5 minutes. Add the beef and cook, crumbling it with a spoon, until no trace of pink remains, about 7 minutes. Spoon off and discard any excess fat. Add the wine, milk, tomato paste, tomatoes, red pepper flakes, oregano, parsley, salt, black pepper, and nutmeg and bring to a simmer. Cover partially, reduce heat, and simmer for 45 minutes. Meanwhile, cook the pasta according to the package directions. Drain and transfer to individual bowls. Top with the sauce and Parmesan.

to freeze...

Omit the pasta and the Parmesan. Let the sauce cool, then ladle it into resealable freezer bags. Store for up to 3 months.

to reheat...

Thaw the sauce overnight in the refrigerator or thaw partially in the microwave. Warm in a covered saucepan over medium-low heat for 20 minutes. Meanwhile, cook the pasta. Spoon the sauce over it and sprinkle with the Parmesan.

•••Tip

Minimize the amount of freezer space taken up by soups, stews, or sauces by freezing them into flat packets. Fill a resealable plastic bag halfway, removing as much air as possible before sealing it. Lay the bag flat on a baking sheet and freeze until solid. Then stand the packet on its side.

freezer meals

BUTTERNUT SQUASH SOUP

hands-on time: 25 minutes | total time: 2 hours | makes 6 to 8 servings

1 3-pound butternut squash
3 tablespoons olive oil
3 teaspoons kosher salt
1/8 teaspoon black pepper
1 tablespoon unsalted butter
1 large yellow onion, chopped
3 celery stalks, chopped
1 tablespoon chopped fresh
 sage leaves
1 32-ounce container low-sodium
 chicken broth

Heat oven to 400° F. Peel and seed the squash. Cut it into 1-inch cubes and place them on a rimmed baking sheet. Drizzle with 2 tablespoons of the oil, 2 teaspoons of the salt, and the pepper and toss to coat. Spread in a single layer and roast for 15 minutes. Turn and continue to roast until softened, about 15 minutes more. Meanwhile, heat the butter and the remaining oil in a stockpot over medium heat. Add the onion, celery, and sage and cook until softened, about 7 minutes. Add the broth, 2 cups of water, the remaining salt, and the squash and bring to a boil. Reduce heat and simmer for 30 minutes. Remove from heat. Let cool for 10 minutes. Working in batches, transfer the soup to a blender and puree until smooth. Return to the pot and warm over medium-low heat.

to freeze...
Let the soup cool, then ladle it into resealable freezer bags. Store for up to 3 months.

to reheat...
Thaw overnight in the refrigerator or thaw partially in the microwave. Warm in a covered saucepan over medium-low heat for 20 minutes.

•••Tip
Roasting the squash before you add it to the soup results in a rich, caramelized flavor. But if you don't have the time, skip this step. Want to save a few more minutes? Look for peeled, cubed butternut squash in the produce section or frozen-vegetable aisle of your supermarket.

MACARONI AND CHEESE

hands-on time: 40 minutes | total time: 1 hour | makes 6 to 8 servings

1 pound dry elbow macaroni

5 tablespoons unsalted butter,
  plus more for the baking dish

1/2 cup all-purpose flour

6 cups whole milk

3 1/2 cups (14 ounces) grated
  sharp Cheddar

3 teaspoons kosher salt

1 cup dry bread crumbs

1/4 cup fresh flat-leaf parsley leaves,
  finely chopped (optional)

1/4 cup olive oil

1/4 teaspoon black pepper

Heat oven to 400° F. Cook the macaroni according to the package directions. Meanwhile, melt the butter in a large saucepan over medium heat. Slowly add the flour. Cook, stirring constantly, for 3 minutes. Add the milk in a steady stream. Cook for 7 minutes. Add the Cheddar and 2 teaspoons of the salt. Cook for 5 minutes. Remove from heat. Add the drained macaroni and toss. Transfer to a buttered casserole or individual ovenproof bowls. Combine the bread crumbs, parsley (if using), oil, pepper, and the remaining salt in a small bowl. Sprinkle over the casserole. Bake until golden and bubbling around the edges, about 25 minutes.

to freeze...

Make the bread-crumb mixture and place it in a resealable freezer bag. Assemble—but do not bake—the casserole. Cover tightly with two layers of foil. Store both for up to 3 months.

to reheat...

Thaw the casserole overnight in the refrigerator or thaw partially in the microwave. Sprinkle the bread-crumb mixture over it. Cover and heat in a 350° F oven for 40 minutes. Uncover and heat until bubbling, about 20 minutes more.

•••Tip

Pasta tends to turn to mush after boiling, freezing, and reheating. Cooking it a couple of minutes shy of the package directions and rinsing it under cool water will help it retain its firmness.

freezer meals

SMOKY SPLIT-PEA SOUP

hands-on time: 15 minutes | total time: 4 hours, 25 minutes | makes 4 to 6 servings

2 ham hocks (about 1 1/2 pounds total)

1 pound green split peas

2 carrots, chopped

2 celery stalks, chopped

1 large yellow onion, chopped

2 cloves garlic, finely chopped

2 32-ounce containers low-sodium
    chicken broth

1 bay leaf

1 tablespoon fresh thyme leaves or
    1 teaspoon dried thyme

Rinse the ham hocks. Place them in a stockpot or Dutch oven along with the remaining ingredients. Bring to a boil. Reduce heat to medium-low, cover, and cook for 3 1/2 to 4 hours. Remove and discard the bay leaf. Transfer the ham hocks to a plate and let cool. When the meat is cool enough to handle, chop or shred it and return it to the soup. Ladle the soup into individual bowls.

to freeze...

Let the soup cool, then ladle it into resealable freezer bags. Store for up to 3 months.

to reheat...

Thaw overnight in the refrigerator or thaw partially in the microwave. Warm the soup in a covered saucepan over medium-low heat for 15 minutes. If the soup seems too thick, stir in up to 1 cup of water to attain the desired consistency.

•••Tip

Look for ham hocks in the meat case, near the bacon. If you can't find them, substitute 1/2 pound of bacon, diced and fried until brown but not crisp, and add an extra pinch of salt.

CHICKEN CURRY

hands-on time: 40 minutes | total time: 1 hour | makes 4 servings

4 tablespoons olive oil
2 medium red onions, cut into
 thin wedges
2 jalapeños, seeded and finely
 chopped
2 cloves garlic, finely chopped
1 2-inch piece fresh ginger,
 thinly sliced
1/4 cup fresh lemon juice
13/4 pounds boneless, skinless
 chicken breasts, cut into
 11/2-inch pieces
1/2 teaspoon cayenne pepper
1/2 teaspoon ground coriander
1/2 teaspoon ground cumin
1/4 teaspoon mustard seeds
1 teaspoon kosher salt
2 ripe yellow peaches,
 roughly chopped (optional)
1/2 cup canned unsweetened
 coconut milk
 Cooked white rice
1/4 cup plain yogurt (optional)

Heat 2 tablespoons of the oil in a large saucepan over medium heat. Add the onions and cook for 5 minutes. Add the jalapeños, garlic, ginger, and lemon juice and cook for 5 minutes. Transfer to a plate. Rinse the chicken and pat it dry with paper towels. Add the remaining oil to the skillet and increase heat to medium-high. Add the chicken and cook until browned but not cooked through, about 4 minutes. Add the cayenne, coriander, cumin, mustard seeds, and salt and stir-fry for 2 minutes. Add the onion mixture, 1/2 cup of water, and the peaches (if using) and simmer for 8 minutes. Add the coconut milk, reduce heat, and simmer for 2 minutes. Spoon the curry into individual bowls. Serve with the rice and yogurt, if desired.

to freeze...
Omit the rice and yogurt. Let the curry cool, then ladle it into resealable freezer bags. Store for up to 3 months.

to reheat...
Thaw the curry overnight in the refrigerator or thaw partially in the microwave. Warm in a covered saucepan over medium-low heat for 20 minutes. Serve with the rice and yogurt, if desired.

••• **Tip**
If you'd rather not buy several different spices, you can use 2 teaspoons of curry powder in place of all the individual flavors.

freezer meals

MUSHROOM BARLEY SOUP

hands-on time: 35 minutes | total time: 45 minutes | makes 4 to 6 servings

1 cup barley

1½ tablespoons olive oil

2 medium yellow onions, chopped

½ teaspoon kosher salt

¼ teaspoon black pepper

1 carrot, chopped

2 celery stalks, chopped

20 ounces button mushrooms, stems trimmed, caps thinly sliced

3 14.5-ounce cans low-sodium chicken or vegetable broth

2 bay leaves

8 sprigs fresh thyme
Sourdough or country bread, toasted (optional)

Bring the barley and 4 cups of water to a boil in a medium saucepan. Reduce heat, cover, and simmer until tender, 30 to 40 minutes. Meanwhile, heat the oil in a large pot over medium-low heat. Add the onions, salt, and pepper. Cook for 5 minutes. Add the carrot and celery and cook for 6 minutes more. Add the mushrooms, increase heat to medium-high, and cook until they release their juices, about 3 minutes. Add the broth, bay leaves, and thyme and simmer for 10 minutes. Stir in the cooked barley and cook for 5 minutes more. Remove and discard the bay leaves and thyme sprigs. Ladle into individual bowls and serve with the toasted bread, if desired.

to freeze...
Let the soup cool, then ladle it into resealable freezer bags. Store for up to 3 months.

to reheat...
Thaw overnight in the refrigerator or thaw partially in the microwave. Warm in a covered saucepan over medium-low heat for 20 minutes. Serve with the toasted bread, if desired.

···•Tip
If you're finding it difficult to extricate food that has been frozen in a plastic bag, use scissors to cut the bag, then simply peel the plastic away.

LASAGNA-STYLE BAKED ZITI

hands-on time: 20 minutes | total time: 45 minutes | makes 4 to 6 servings

1 pound dry ziti

1 tablespoon olive oil

1 large yellow onion, chopped

3/4 teaspoon kosher salt

1/4 teaspoon black pepper

1 pound ground beef

3 cloves garlic, finely chopped

1/2 cup chopped fresh oregano
  or 1 1/2 tablespoons dried oregano
  (optional)

1 24- to 26-ounce jar pasta sauce

1 15-ounce container ricotta

1 10-ounce box frozen spinach,
  thawed and squeezed to remove
  excess moisture

1/2 cup (2 ounces) grated Parmesan

1 cup (4 ounces) shredded
  mozzarella

Heat oven to 400° F. Cook the ziti according to the package directions. Meanwhile, heat the oil in a large pot over medium heat. Add the onion, salt, and pepper and cook for 5 minutes. Add the beef and cook, crumbling it with a spoon, until no trace of pink remains, about 7 minutes. Spoon off and discard any excess fat. Add the garlic and oregano (if using) and cook for 2 minutes. Add the pasta sauce and cook for 3 minutes. Remove from heat. Add the drained ziti to the pot and toss. Add the ricotta, spinach, and 1/4 cup of the Parmesan and toss again. Spread the mixture into a 9-by-13-inch baking dish. Sprinkle with the mozzarella and the remaining Parmesan. Bake until the mozzarella melts, about 15 minutes.

to freeze...

Assemble—but do not bake—the casserole. Cover tightly with two layers of aluminum foil. Store for up to 3 months.

to reheat...

Thaw overnight in the refrigerator or thaw partially in the microwave. Cover and heat in a 350° F oven for 1 hour. Uncover and heat until the mozzarella melts, about 10 minutes more.

••• Tip

Don't allow your baking dish to be taken hostage by a frozen casserole. Before placing food in the dish, line it with several layers of foil. After freezing, lift the foil and food from the dish and wrap it tightly in plastic wrap. When you are ready to thaw the food, remove the plastic wrap and foil and return the icy block to its dish.

freezer meals

MEATBALLS

hands-on time: 30 minutes | total time: 1 hour | makes 8 servings

2 pounds ground beef
1/2 medium yellow onion, finely chopped
1 slice white bread, crust trimmed, torn into small pieces
3 cloves garlic, finely chopped
1 large egg
1/4 cup fresh flat-leaf parsley leaves, chopped
2 tablespoons olive oil
1 1/2 teaspoons Italian seasoning
1 1/2 teaspoons kosher salt
3/4 cup (3 ounces) grated Parmesan
1 1/2 teaspoons black pepper
3/4 cup ricotta
1 24- to 26-ounce jar pasta sauce, warmed

Heat oven to 400° F. In a large bowl, combine the beef, onion, bread, garlic, egg, parsley, oil, Italian seasoning, salt, 1/2 cup of the Parmesan, and 1 teaspoon of the pepper. Shape the mixture into 16 meatballs (about 1/3 cup each). Place them on a rimmed baking sheet. Bake for 25 minutes. Meanwhile, in a separate bowl, combine the ricotta and the remaining Parmesan and pepper; set aside. Remove the meatballs from oven and turn on broiler. Spoon a few teaspoons of the ricotta mixture onto each meatball. Broil until the ricotta browns, 3 to 5 minutes. Serve on top of the warmed pasta sauce.

to freeze...
Omit the ricotta mixture. Place the baked meatballs on a baking sheet and freeze for at least 1 hour. Transfer to resealable freezer bags and return to the freezer. Store for up to 3 months.

to reheat...
Thaw the meatballs overnight in the refrigerator or thaw partially in the microwave. Place them in a baking dish, cover with foil, and heat in a 350° F oven for 20 minutes. Top with the ricotta mixture and broil as described above. Serve on top of the warmed pasta sauce.

···Tip
To save a few calories, bake the meatballs on a wire rack placed on a rimmed baking sheet. Any excess fat will end up dripping onto the pan.

PASTA AND BEANS

hands-on time: 15 minutes | total time: 2 hours (includes soaking) | makes 6 to 8 servings

1 16-ounce bag dried cannellini or
    navy beans
1 large yellow onion, finely chopped
2 celery stalks, finely chopped
5 cloves garlic, finely chopped
1 tablespoon chopped fresh sage leaves
    or 1 teaspoon dried sage
1 tablespoon finely chopped
    fresh rosemary or 1 teaspoon
    dried rosemary
1 14.5-ounce can low-sodium
    chicken broth
1 14.5-ounce can diced tomatoes,
    undrained
1 cup dry small pasta, such as
    ditalini or tubettini
1 tablespoon kosher salt
1 tablespoon black pepper
1/4 teaspoon red pepper flakes
1 tablespoon extra-virgin olive oil
    Shaved Parmesan

Bring the beans and 6 cups of water to a boil in a Dutch oven or stockpot. Cook, stirring occasionally, for 5 minutes. Remove from heat, cover, and let soak for 45 minutes. Drain the beans and return them to the pot. Add the onion, celery, garlic, sage, rosemary, broth, and 10 cups of water. Bring to a boil. Reduce heat to a simmer. Cook, stirring occasionally, until the beans are tender, 30 to 40 minutes. Add the tomatoes and cook for 10 minutes. Add the pasta, salt, black pepper, and red pepper flakes. Cook until the pasta is al dente, 5 to 7 minutes. Ladle the soup into bowls, drizzle with the oil, and sprinkle with the Parmesan.

to freeze...
Omit the pasta, oil, and Parmesan. Let the soup cool, then ladle it into resealable freezer bags. Store for up to 3 months.

to reheat...
Thaw the soup overnight in the refrigerator. Warm in a covered saucepan over medium-low heat for 20 minutes. Uncover and bring to a simmer. Add the pasta and cook for 5 to 7 minutes more. Drizzle with the oil and sprinkle with the Parmesan.

•••Tip
Small pasta shapes are ideal for soup because they cook quickly and don't overwhelm the other ingredients. If you can't find them in your supermarket, substitute an equal amount of spaghetti broken into small pieces.

freezer meals

CHEESY VEGETABLE PASTA

hands-on time: 25 minutes | total time: 1 hour, 20 minutes | makes 4 servings

1/2 pound dry ziti or penne

1 tablespoon balsamic vinegar

3/4 teaspoon kosher salt

1/4 cup olive oil

2 medium zucchini, halved lengthwise

2 medium eggplants, halved lengthwise

1/2 large yellow onion, quartered

2 large cloves garlic, finely chopped

1 1/2 teaspoons fresh oregano or 1/2 teaspoon dried oregano

4 plum tomatoes, chopped

1 cup pasta sauce

3/4 cup (3 ounces) crumbled Feta

1/4 teaspoon black pepper

1/2 teaspoon red pepper flakes

2 cups (8 ounces) shredded mozzarella

Cook the pasta according to the package directions. Meanwhile, whisk together the vinegar, 1/2 teaspoon of the salt, and 1 tablespoon of the oil in a small bowl. Place the zucchini, eggplants, and onion on a baking sheet. Brush with the vinaigrette. Heat broiler on high. Broil until tender, 8 minutes per side. Heat oven to 350° F. Chop the roasted vegetables. Place a large pot over low heat. Add the garlic and the remaining oil and cook for 3 minutes. Add the drained pasta, vegetables, oregano, tomatoes, pasta sauce, Feta, black pepper, red pepper flakes, and the remaining salt and toss. Transfer to a 9-by-13-inch baking dish. Sprinkle with the mozzarella. Cover and bake for 30 minutes. Uncover and bake for 20 minutes more.

to freeze...
Assemble—but do not bake—the casserole. Cover tightly with two layers of aluminum foil. Store for up to 3 months.

to reheat...
Thaw overnight in the refrigerator or thaw partially in the microwave. Cover and heat in a 350° F oven for 30 minutes. Uncover and heat for 10 minutes more.

•••Tip
To make individual servings, freeze the pasta in ramekins or small ovenproof bowls. Cover and heat for 20 minutes, then uncover and heat for 10 minutes more.

CLASSIC BEEF STEW

hands-on time: 35 minutes | total time: 4 hours, 30 minutes | makes 8 to 10 servings

4 pounds bottom round, trimmed and cut into 2-inch pieces, or 4 pounds precut stew meat

1 cup all-purpose flour

1/3 cup olive oil

2 large yellow onions, chopped

1 6-ounce can tomato paste

1 cup dry red wine

1 pound Yukon gold potatoes, cut into 2-inch pieces (peel first, if desired)

8 ounces baby-cut carrots

1 14.5-ounce can beef broth

1 tablespoon kosher salt

1 tablespoon fresh thyme leaves or 1 teaspoon dried thyme

1 bay leaf

1 cup frozen peas, thawed

Heat oven to 350° F. Lightly coat the beef in the flour. Heat 3 tablespoons of the oil in a Dutch oven over medium-high heat. Add some of the beef to the pot, being careful not to crowd the pieces. Cook until browned, about 7 minutes per side. Transfer to a plate; set aside. Repeat with the remaining oil and beef. Reduce heat to medium, add the onions, and cook for 10 minutes. Add the tomato paste and stir. Add the wine and cook, stirring to scrape up any browned bits, for 1 minute. Add the beef, potatoes, carrots, broth, salt, thyme, and bay leaf. Cover and bring to a boil. Transfer to oven. Cook until the beef is tender, 2 to 2 1/2 hours. Remove and discard the bay leaf. Add the peas and cook over medium-high heat for 3 minutes. Ladle into individual bowls.

to freeze...
Omit the peas. Let the stew cool, then ladle it into resealable freezer bags. Store for up to 3 months.

to reheat...
Thaw the stew overnight in the refrigerator or thaw partially in the microwave. Warm in a covered saucepan over medium-low heat for about 20 minutes, adding the peas during the last 5 minutes.

•••**Tip**

For a leaner dish, refrigerate the stew overnight before serving or freezing. The fat will rise to the surface and solidify, making it easy to skim and discard.

freezer meals

TURKEY NOODLE SOUP

hands-on time: 25 minutes | total time: 3 hours, 45 minutes | makes 6 servings

1 carcass from a 12- to 14-
pound turkey

1 large yellow onion, quartered

2 teaspoons kosher salt

6 whole black peppercorns

2 sprigs fresh tarragon,
plus 2 tablespoons chopped
tarragon leaves

5 carrots, peeled

5 celery stalks

1 handful celery leaves, chopped
(optional)

8 ounces wide egg noodles

3 cups cooked turkey, cut into
1-inch chunks

1/2 teaspoon black pepper

Place the turkey carcass, onion, salt, peppercorns, and tarragon sprigs in a large pot. Halve 3 of the carrots and 3 of the celery stalks and add them to the pot. Add enough water to cover (about 14 cups). Bring to a boil. Reduce heat, cover partially, and simmer for 1 1/2 hours. Uncover and simmer for 1 to 1 1/2 more hours. Strain the stock, discarding the solids, then return it to the pot. Chop the remaining carrots and celery. Add them to the pot with the celery leaves (if using). Bring to a boil. Add the noodles and cook for 6 minutes. Reduce heat, add the chopped tarragon leaves and turkey meat, and simmer for 5 minutes. Add the pepper and ladle into individual bowls.

to freeze...
Omit the egg noodles. Let the soup cool, then ladle it into resealable plastic freezer bags. Store for up to 3 months.

to reheat...
Thaw the soup overnight in the refrigerator or thaw partially in the microwave. Warm in a covered saucepan over medium-low heat for 20 minutes. Uncover and bring to a simmer. Add the egg noodles and cook for 11 minutes more.

••• Tip

When chopping vegetables for your Thanksgiving meal, chop a few extra, place them in plastic bags, and refrigerate them. That way your prep work will be nearly nil when it comes time to make the soup with that leftover turkey.

CHAPTER SIX

shortcut meals

Generally speaking, cheating (on tests, at Scrabble) is wrong. But cheating in the kitchen? That's another story altogether. When you need to put dinner on the table pronto, it's perfectly acceptable to enlist convenience foods like rotisserie chicken, jarred pasta sauce, or even frozen toaster waffles as accomplices—if it means you can skip a step (or ten) in the process. To cover your tracks, all you have to do is add a few other ingredients. And if a trace of guilt still lingers, take comfort: The resulting dishes taste just like homemade, so there's no penalty if you get caught.

CHICKEN POTPIE

hands-on time: 35 minutes | total time: 1 hour, 35 minutes | makes 6 servings

1 stick unsalted butter

5 tablespoons all-purpose flour, plus more for rolling the crust

4 cups low-sodium chicken broth

1 large yellow onion, chopped

2 tablespoons fresh thyme leaves or 2 teaspoons dried thyme

4 carrots, chopped

1 10-ounce package button mushrooms, stems trimmed and caps quartered

1½ teaspoons kosher salt

¾ teaspoon black pepper

1 store-bought rotisserie chicken, meat shredded

1 10-ounce package frozen peas

1 store-bought piecrust

Heat oven to 425° F. Melt 5 tablespoons of the butter in a medium saucepan over medium heat. Whisking constantly, slowly add the flour and cook for 3 minutes. Still whisking, slowly add the broth. Bring to a boil. Reduce heat and simmer until thickened slightly, about 5 minutes. Remove from heat. Melt 2 tablespoons of the remaining butter in a skillet over medium heat. Add the onion and cook until softened, about 7 minutes. Add the thyme and carrots and cook for 5 minutes more. Transfer to a 9-by-13-inch baking dish. Melt the remaining butter in the skillet over medium-high heat. Add the mushrooms and cook for 2 minutes. Reduce heat, season with ½ teaspoon of the salt and ¼ teaspoon of the pepper, and simmer until the liquid evaporates, about 3 minutes. Add the mushrooms to the dish along with the chicken, peas, the reserved sauce, and the remaining salt and pepper and toss. Roll out the piecrust on a floured surface until it is slightly larger than the dish. Lay it on top and tuck under any dough that hangs over the edges. Cut two 2-inch slits in the crust. Bake until the crust is golden brown, about 20 minutes. Reduce heat to 350° F and bake until the filling starts to bubble, 25 minutes more.

•••Tip

To cut down on last-minute prep, assemble this dish early in the day and refrigerate it, then bake it just before serving.

shortcut meals

SHRIMP FRA DIAVOLO

hands-on time: 5 minutes | total time: 20 minutes | makes 4 servings

1 pound dry spaghetti, fettuccine,
or linguine

1 1-pound bag frozen uncooked
shrimp, thawed

2 tablespoons olive oil

1 24- to 26-ounce jar pasta sauce

1/2 to 1 teaspoon red pepper flakes
or hot sauce

Cook the pasta according to the package directions. Meanwhile, rinse the shrimp and pat them dry with paper towels. Heat the oil in a large skillet over medium-high heat. Add the shrimp and cook, turning once, until pink and cooked through, about 4 minutes total. Transfer to a plate. Add the pasta sauce to the skillet and cook until heated through. Drain the pasta and return it to the pot. Add the pasta sauce, shrimp, and pepper flakes or hot sauce to the pot and toss. Place over low heat until warmed through, about 1 minute.

and the next time, try...
Varying the flavor with a few kitchen staples:
• Sauté some garlic or onions, or both, in the oil before adding the shrimp.
• Stir in a pinch of grated orange zest and crushed fennel seeds when you heat the sauce.
• Drop in a handful of chopped green or black olives before tossing the pasta.

••• Tip
Defrost shrimp on the double by putting them in a colander and placing it in the sink under cool running water for a few minutes.

shortcut meals

ANTIPASTO PLATE

hands-on time: 15 minutes | total time: 15 minutes | makes 6 servings

1 pound fresh mozzarella bocconcini or two 8-ounce balls fresh mozzarella

1 6-ounce package thinly sliced salami

2 4-ounce packages bresaola

12 ounces Parmesan

2 5-ounce bags arugula

1 12- to 16-ounce jar roasted red peppers, drained and roughly chopped

1 12-ounce jar giardiniera, drained (optional)

1/2 cup extra-virgin olive oil

3 tablespoons red wine vinegar

1/4 teaspoon kosher salt

1/4 teaspoon black pepper

Cut the mozzarella, salami, and bresaola into 1-inch pieces. Crumble the Parmesan into small chunks. Place 1 large handful of the arugula on each plate. Arrange some of the mozzarella, salami, bresaola, Parmesan, roasted peppers, and giardiniera (if using) on top. Drizzle first with the oil and then with the vinegar. Season with the salt and pepper to taste. Toss gently.

and the next time, try...
Using any or all of the colorful items you find in your local Italian deli: prosciutto, Pecorino, olives, marinated artichokes or mushrooms, caper berries, soppressata, pepperoncini...

••• Tip

Giardiniera are pickled vegetables. You can find them next to the pickles and olives in supermarkets and specialty stores. Bocconcini, small balls of fresh mozzarella, are available at some specialty cheese counters. Bresaola is thinly sliced, salted, air-dried aged beef and is sold in Italian delis and specialty stores.

shortcut meals

INSIDE-OUT SPRING ROLLS

hands-on time: 15 minutes | total time: 15 minutes | makes 4 servings

1 16-ounce bag frozen pot stickers
1 tablespoon olive or peanut oil
1 carrot, thinly sliced on the diagonal
1 small head Napa cabbage,
   thinly sliced
2 tablespoons low-sodium soy sauce
1/4 cup salted peanuts

Fry the pot stickers according to the package directions. Meanwhile, heat the oil in a nonstick skillet over medium-high heat. Add the carrot and cabbage and toss to coat. Add the soy sauce and cook for 2 to 3 minutes. To serve, transfer the vegetables to individual bowls, top with the pot stickers, and sprinkle with the peanuts.

and the next time, try...
Making your life even easier by substituting 3 cups of packaged slaw mix (found in the produce section of most supermarkets) for the sliced carrot and cabbage.

••• Tip
Napa cabbage (also known as Chinese cabbage) has thinner, more crinkly leaves than standard green cabbage and is much milder in flavor. But if you can't find Napa cabbage at your supermarket, it's perfectly fine to use green cabbage in its place.

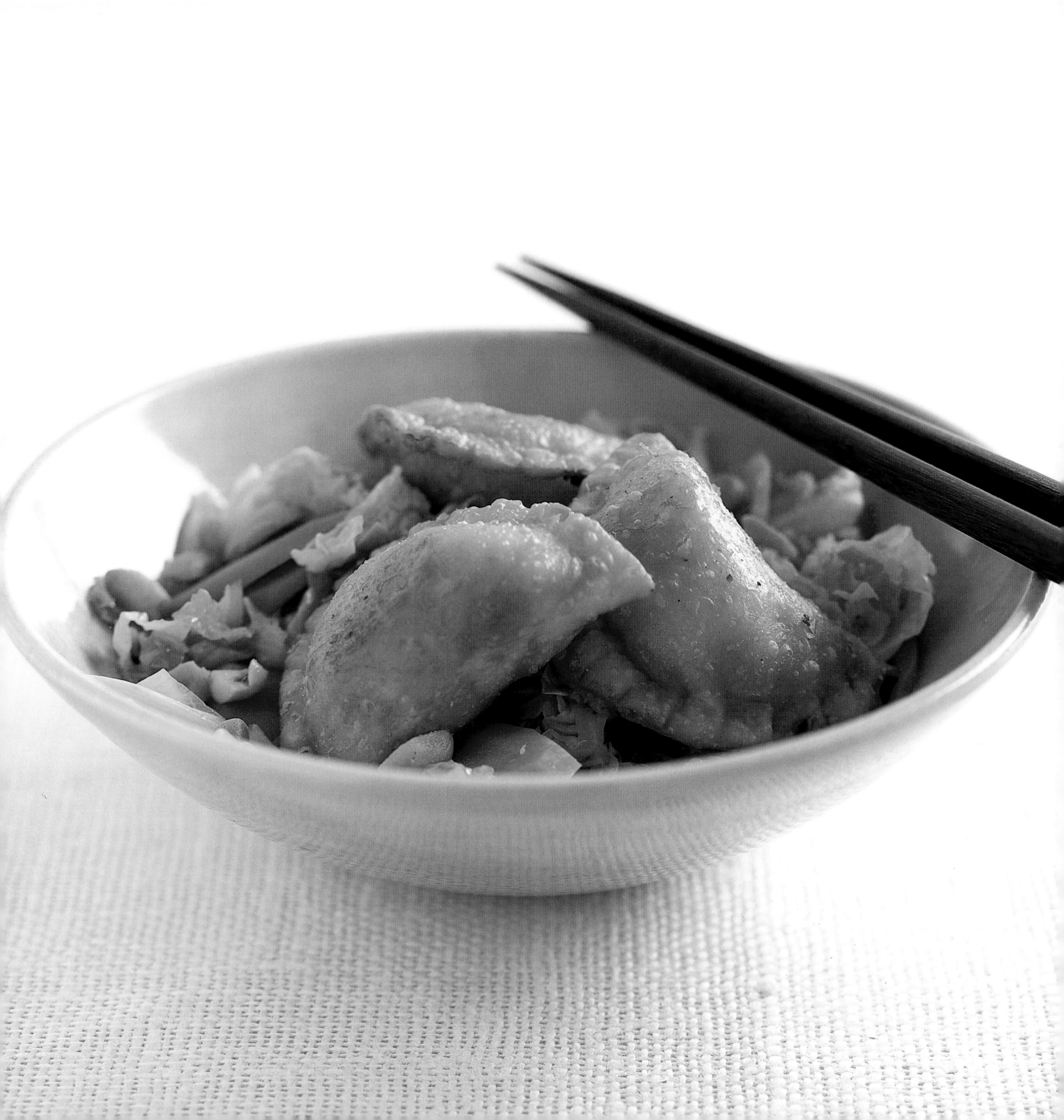

MEATBALL HEROES

hands-on time: 15 minutes | total time: 15 minutes | makes 4 servings

    4 submarine rolls
    1 teaspoon olive oil
   12 to 20 frozen or refrigerated
       precooked meatballs
    1 14- to 16-ounce jar pasta sauce
    1 8-ounce bag shredded mozzarella
  1/2 cup (2 ounces) grated Parmesan
       Pickle spears (optional)

Heat oven to 250° F. Warm the rolls on the oven rack. Meanwhile, heat the oil in a large skillet over medium heat. Add the meatballs and cook until browned on all sides, 3 to 5 minutes total. Add the sauce, reduce heat, and simmer for 3 minutes. Halve each roll lengthwise. Spoon some of the meatballs and sauce onto the bottom half of each roll and sprinkle with the mozzarella and Parmesan. Sandwich with the top half of each roll. Serve with the pickles, if desired.

••• Tip

You can find precooked meatballs in most supermarkets. But if you want ones that taste just as good as Grandma's, head to an Italian deli.

shortcut meals

LAST-MINUTE LASAGNA

hands-on time: 10 minutes | total time: 45 minutes | makes 6 servings

1 24- to 26-ounce jar pasta sauce
2 16- to 18-ounce bags frozen large
  cheese ravioli, unthawed
1 10-ounce box frozen chopped
  spinach, thawed and squeezed
  to remove excess water
1 8-ounce bag shredded mozzarella
1/2 cup (2 ounces) grated Parmesan

Heat oven to 350° F. Spoon 1/3 of the pasta sauce into a 9-by-13-inch baking dish. Place half of the ravioli on top of the sauce in a single layer. Sprinkle with the spinach and half of the mozzarella. Layer on the remaining ravioli (you may not need all of them). Top with the remaining sauce and mozzarella and the Parmesan. Cover with foil and bake for 25 minutes. Uncover and bake until bubbling, 5 to 10 minutes more.

••• Tip
Frozen spinach contains a lot of water, which, if not removed, can ruin a recipe. To extract the excess moisture, place the thawed block of spinach in a colander to drain, then press down on it or squeeze it with your hands.

SESAME CHICKEN SALAD

hands-on time: 15 minutes | total time: 15 minutes | makes 4 servings

2 carrots
2 5-ounce bags baby spinach
1 small red onion, thinly sliced
3 tablespoons sesame seeds, toasted
1 store-bought rotisserie chicken,
  meat shredded
1 1-inch piece fresh ginger, grated
2 tablespoons low-sodium soy sauce
2 tablespoons rice vinegar
1/4 cup sesame oil

Using a vegetable peeler, shave the carrots into long, thin ribbons. In a large bowl, combine the carrots, spinach, onion, sesame seeds, and chicken. In a separate bowl, whisk together the ginger, soy sauce, and vinegar. Whisking constantly, slowly add the oil in a steady stream. Pour the vinaigrette over the salad and toss to coat. Divide among individual plates and serve.

and the next time, try...
Assembling this salad with shredded lettuce in place of the baby spinach for a crunchier texture—and a more kid-friendly taste.

•••Tip
Toasting brings out the nutty flavor of sesame seeds. Heat them in a dry skillet over medium heat, stirring the seeds or shaking the pan frequently, for 1 to 2 minutes. Watch the seeds carefully; they can go from lightly toasted to scorched in seconds.

shortcut meals

SHRIMP WITH ARUGULA AND COUSCOUS

hands-on time: 15 minutes | total time: 15 minutes | makes 4 servings

1 cup instant couscous

3/4 teaspoon kosher salt

1/8 teaspoon black pepper

3 tablespoons olive oil

1 clove garlic, thinly sliced

1 5-ounce bag arugula

1 1-pound bag frozen uncooked shrimp, thawed

1 lemon, cut into wedges

Prepare the couscous according to the package directions. After cooking, season it with 1/4 teaspoon of the salt and a pinch of the pepper. Meanwhile, heat 2 tablespoons of the oil in a large skillet over medium heat. Add the garlic and cook for 1 minute. Add the arugula and cook just until wilted, about 1 minute. Transfer to a plate. Rinse the shrimp and pat them dry with paper towels. Heat the remaining oil in the skillet over medium-high heat. Add the shrimp, lemon wedges, and the remaining salt and pepper. Cook, turning once, until the shrimp are pink and cooked through, about 4 minutes total. Return the garlic and arugula to the skillet and toss. Serve over the couscous.

••• Tip

Arugula has a peppery flavor and a fairly hearty texture that stand up well to a brief stint in the skillet. If you prefer something a little milder in flavor, try spinach.

shortcut meals

FRENCH FRY PIE

hands-on time: 15 minutes | total time: 40 minutes | makes 4 servings

1 28-ounce package frozen
   shoestring French fries
1 1/2 pounds ground beef
1 14- to 16-ounce jar pasta sauce
1/2 teaspoon kosher salt

Heat oven to 425° F. Spread the fries on a baking sheet. Bake until golden, about 25 minutes. Meanwhile, cook the beef in a medium saucepan over medium heat, crumbling it with a spoon, until no trace of pink remains, about 7 minutes. Spoon off and discard any excess fat. Stir in the pasta sauce and cook until warmed through, about 5 minutes. Transfer to an 8-inch-square baking dish or a 9-inch deep-dish pie plate. Top with the fries and return to oven for 5 to 10 minutes. Season with the salt. Spoon into individual bowls.

••• Tip

Is dinner ready before your family is? Like most casseroles, the French Fry Pie can remain in the oven for at least 15 additional minutes while everyone meanders to the table.

shortcut meals

MEDITERRANEAN CHICKEN

hands-on time: 20 minutes | total time: 30 minutes | makes 4 servings

1/2 cup (2 ounces) crumbled Feta

4 tablespoons black-olive
   tapenade or paste

4 boneless, skinless chicken breast
   halves

1/2 teaspoon black pepper

3 tablespoons olive oil

1/2 cup store-bought salsa (preferably
   fresh), drained

1 5-ounce bag baby spinach

4 tablespoons capers (optional)

1 lemon, cut into wedges

Heat oven to 375° F. Combine the Feta and tapenade in a small bowl. Rinse the chicken and pat it dry with paper towels. With a sharp knife, make a 2-inch slit in the thickest part of each chicken breast half to form a pocket. Using a spoon, stuff some of the Feta mixture into each pocket. Season the chicken with the pepper. Heat 2 tablespoons of the oil in a nonstick skillet over medium heat. Add the chicken and cook until browned, about 2 minutes per side. Transfer to a baking dish and bake until cooked through, about 15 minutes. Meanwhile, heat the remaining oil and the salsa in the skillet over medium heat until warmed through, about 5 minutes. Add the spinach and cook, tossing frequently, until barely wilted, about 1 minute. Place the spinach and salsa on individual plates, top with the chicken, and sprinkle with the capers, if desired. Serve the lemon wedges on the side.

••• Tip

If you don't have enough chicken on hand to serve everyone an individual piece, cut the chicken crosswise into slices and fan them out on the plates. No one will know the difference.

HAM-AND-CHEESE WAFFLE SANDWICHES

hands-on time: 10 minutes | total time: 20 minutes | makes 4 servings

8 frozen plain or whole-grain toaster
waffles, unthawed

1 tablespoon Dijon mustard (optional)

1/2 pound sliced deli ham

1/4 pound Cheddar, thinly sliced

4 tablespoons unsalted butter

Place 4 of the waffles on a work surface. Spread with the mustard (if using). Top with the ham, Cheddar, and the remaining waffles. Spread the top of each sandwich with 1/2 tablespoon of the butter. Melt the remaining butter in a large non-stick skillet over medium heat. Place the sandwiches in the skillet, buttered-side up. Cook, pressing with the back of a spatula and turning occasionally, until the Cheddar melts and the waffles are golden, 3 to 4 minutes per side.

and the next time, try...
Switching up the fillings with other pantry and refrigerator staples:
• Turkey, mozzarella, and honey mustard
• Peanut butter and jelly
• Scrambled eggs and Swiss cheese

••• Tip

Looking to get some mileage out of your neglected waffle iron? Use it to put a new face— a dimpled one at that— on sandwiches made with plain sliced bread.

shortcut meals

SPICY CHICKEN AND TORTILLA SOUP

hands-on time: 20 minutes │ total time: 40 minutes │ makes 4 servings

1 store-bought rotisserie chicken
2 32-ounce containers low-
   sodium chicken broth
1 small red onion, finely chopped
2 jalapeños, seeded and thinly sliced
2 large tomatoes, seeded and diced
1 cup corn kernels, thawed if frozen, or
   fresh (from 2 ears)
   A couple of handfuls of tortilla chips
1/2 cup fresh cilantro leaves
1 ripe avocado, roughly chopped
1 cup (4 ounces) crumbled Feta
1 lime, cut into wedges

Remove and discard the skin from the chicken. Place the entire chicken and the broth in a large pot over medium heat. Simmer for 20 minutes. Transfer the chicken to a plate to cool. Strain the broth into another saucepan. Shred the chicken meat and add it to the broth, along with the onion, jalapeños, and tomatoes and their juices. Place over medium heat and cook for 5 minutes. Add the corn and heat until warmed through, about 3 minutes. Place some of the tortilla chips in each bowl. Ladle in the soup and top with the cilantro, avocado, Feta, and the remaining chips. Serve the lime wedges on the side.

••• Tip

Among hot peppers, jalapeños fall in the medium-spicy range. If you prefer something certifiably hot, substitute serrano or Thai red chili peppers.

CHAPTER SEVEN

reliable sides

The ideal dinner companion is easy to get along with, uncomplicated but interesting, and at home in any situation—no matter how formal, casual, or chaotic. While this may not always describe the people seated *at* your table, at least it can apply to what's *on* the table when you serve one of the side dishes in this chapter. Not only are they exceptionally likable and charmingly versatile but they're also well-behaved enough to master the first time around. Meaning you'll invite them back again and again.

BUTTERMILK MASHED POTATOES

hands-on time: 15 minutes | total time: 30 minutes | makes 6 servings

3/4 pound Yukon gold or russet
   potatoes, peeled and quartered
2 teaspoons kosher salt
4 tablespoons unsalted butter
1 cup buttermilk
1/4 teaspoon black pepper
1/8 teaspoon grated nutmeg

Place the potatoes and 1 teaspoon of the salt in a large pot. Add enough cold water to cover. Bring to a boil. Reduce heat and simmer until the potatoes are fork-tender, about 15 minutes. Drain the potatoes and return them to the pot. Meanwhile, heat the butter and buttermilk in a small saucepan over medium heat until bubbles appear. Add to the potatoes and mash. Season with the pepper, nutmeg, and the remaining salt.

and the next time, try...
Stirring in a little something extra at the end:
• Grated Cheddar (1/2 cup should do the trick)
• Chopped fresh herbs, such as thyme, parsley, basil, dill, or tarragon
• Defrosted frozen peas

•••Tip

If you value 10 minutes of your time more than a smooth mash, don't peel the potatoes. Thin-skinned varieties like Yukon golds can squeak by with just a good scrub. The colorful flecks of peel will lend the resulting puree a little character—and give you a chance to read the mail.

reliable sides

BROCCOLI RABE WITH OLIVES AND LEMON

hands-on time: 10 minutes | total time: 25 minutes | makes 4 servings

1 pound broccoli rabe, trimmed
1 tablespoon olive oil
1 tablespoon unsalted butter
2 cloves garlic, thinly sliced
1 lemon, halved and seeded
1/3 cup green olives, pitted and roughly chopped if desired
1/4 teaspoon kosher salt
1/8 teaspoon black pepper

Bring a large pot of salted water to a boil. Add the broccoli rabe and cook until almost tender but still crisp, about 3 minutes. Drain. Meanwhile, heat the oil and butter in a large skillet over medium heat. Add the garlic and cook until golden, about 1 minute. Carefully squeeze half the lemon over the butter mixture. Cut the squeezed lemon half into wedges and toss them into the skillet. Add the broccoli rabe, olives, salt, and pepper and heat for 2 minutes. Cut the remaining lemon half into wedges and serve on the side.

and the next time, try...
Sweetening the dish up with dried fruit. Just add one of the following to the skillet along with the broccoli rabe (a handful should do):
• Currants
• Golden raisins
• Dried cherries
• Dried cranberries

•••Tip
Salt the cooking water when you boil vegetables to help bring out their natural flavor. Add just enough so the water tastes briny, like the sea. (Skip the salt when boiling corn, though—it makes the corn tough.)

YELLOW WAX BEANS WITH TOASTED ALMONDS

hands-on time: 10 minutes | total time: 15 minutes | makes 6 servings

1 pound yellow wax beans

2 tablespoons olive oil

2 tablespoons unsalted butter

3/4 cup whole blanched almonds, coarsely chopped

1/2 teaspoon kosher salt

1/4 teaspoon black pepper

Bring a large pot of salted water to a boil. Add the beans and cook until tender, 3 to 5 minutes. Drain the beans and transfer them to a bowl of ice water. Drain them again and place in a serving dish. Heat the oil and butter in a large skillet over medium heat. Add the almonds and cook, stirring, until they turn golden but not brown, about 2 minutes. Transfer the almonds to the dish with the beans, add the salt and pepper, and toss.

and the next time, try...
Raiding your freezer and substituting frozen green beans for the fresh yellow wax beans.

••• Tip
When you toast nuts or seeds, remove them from the skillet as soon as they are golden. Otherwise the residual heat of the pan will continue to brown—and possibly burn—them.

reliable sides

CANDIED CARROTS

hands-on time: 10 minutes | total time: 30 minutes | makes 6 servings

4 tablespoons unsalted butter
1/4 cup maple syrup
1/4 teaspoon kosher salt
1/8 teaspoon cayenne pepper
1 1/2 pounds carrots, halved lengthwise
1/8 teaspoon black pepper

Melt the butter in a large saucepan over medium heat. Add the maple syrup, salt, cayenne, and 1/4 cup of water and bring to a boil. Add the carrots and return to a boil. Reduce heat and simmer, turning occasionally, until the carrots are tender and the liquid has reduced to a glaze, 15 to 20 minutes. Season with the black pepper.

and the next time, try...
Playing with the ratio of heat to sweet. Omit the cayenne and just use plenty of black pepper. Or skip the cayenne and black pepper altogether.

••• Tip
Long, slender carrots make for a beautiful-looking dish, but unsliced baby-cut carrots will taste just as delicious— and save you some time and effort.

MINTED PEAS

hands-on time: 10 minutes | total time: 20 minutes | makes 4 servings

1 10-ounce package frozen peas

1 tablespoon unsalted butter

1/2 teaspoon kosher salt

1/8 teaspoon black pepper

1 teaspoon fresh lemon juice

2 tablespoons chopped fresh
   mint leaves

Bring a large pot of salted water to a boil. Add the peas and cook until tender, 3 to 5 minutes. Drain. Heat the butter in a large skillet over medium heat. Add the peas, salt, pepper, and lemon juice. Cook until warmed through, about 2 minutes. Remove from heat. Add the mint and toss.

and the next time, try...
Taking advantage of what's in your freezer (or on your countertop): Try ripped basil leaves in place of the mint, or trade in the frozen peas for frozen snow peas or sugar snap peas.

••• Tip
If you'd rather not have peas skittering all over (and off) your kids' plates, parlay this side dish into a puree that stays put. Just grab a potato masher or the back of a wooden spoon and smash the peas right in the skillet.

reliable sides

ROASTED TOMATOES

hands-on time: 10 minutes | total time: 40 minutes (includes cooling) | makes 4 servings

2 pints cherry or grape tomatoes

2 tablespoons extra-virgin
   olive oil, plus more for drizzling
   if desired

1/2 teaspoon kosher salt

1/4 teaspoon black pepper

10 sprigs fresh thyme

Heat oven to 425° F. Arrange the tomatoes in a single layer on a rimmed baking sheet or in a baking dish. Drizzle with the oil and season with the salt and pepper. Scatter the thyme over the top. Roast until the tomatoes are softened, 15 to 20 minutes. Let cool at least 10 minutes before serving. If desired, drizzle with more oil.

and the next time, try...
Embellishing the flavor:
• Toss in some thinly sliced garlic, whole
   kalamata olives, or both, prior to roasting.
• Sprinkle with thinly sliced basil instead
   of the thyme (add it when you remove the
   tomatoes from the oven).
• Drizzle on balsamic vinegar along with
   the oil just before serving.

••• Tip
Do you really have to let the tomatoes cool before serving? The answer is yes, if you really want to taste their sweet flavor.

168

CREAMY PARMESAN POLENTA

hands-on time: 5 minutes | total time: 10 minutes | makes 4 servings

1 tablespoon kosher salt
1 cup instant polenta
1/2 cup (2 ounces) grated Parmesan
4 tablespoons unsalted butter

Bring 4 cups of water and the salt to a boil in a saucepan. Stirring constantly, slowly add the polenta. Cook, still stirring constantly, until the polenta thickens, about 3 minutes. Remove from heat and stir in the Parmesan and butter. Cover and set aside until the butter melts, about 2 minutes. Stir again before serving.

and the next time, try...
Making a double batch—after all, the best thing about polenta is the leftovers. Pour the unused polenta into a square baking dish and refrigerate it overnight. Then slice it and fry it in butter or olive oil until it's golden brown on both sides. Sprinkle with coarsely ground black pepper or drizzle with maple syrup, if desired.

•••**Tip**
Resist the urge to stop stirring the polenta midway or lumps will inevitably appear. And once they show up, they're there to stay.

reliable sides

ASPARAGUS WITH SOY DRESSING

hands-on time: 10 minutes | total time: 15 minutes | makes 4 servings

1 teaspoon kosher salt
1 large bunch asparagus, trimmed
1/4 cup low-sodium soy sauce
1/4 cup fresh lemon juice
2 tablespoons rice vinegar
2 1/2 tablespoons rice wine, sherry,
　　or white wine
1 tablespoon sugar
2 teaspoons sesame oil
1 clove garlic, thinly sliced

Pour about 2 inches of water into a large saucepan. Add the salt and bring to a boil. Add the asparagus, cover, and cook until tender, 3 to 7 minutes. (The time will vary depending on the size of the stalks.) Drain and transfer to a platter. Meanwhile, in a separate saucepan, over medium heat, bring the remaining ingredients plus 2 tablespoons of water to a simmer, stirring until the sugar dissolves. Cook for 3 to 5 minutes. Spoon the dressing over the asparagus; cover and refrigerate any leftover dressing to use on another night.

and the next time, try...
Drizzling the leftover dressing over any green vegetable you stumble across at the farmers' market or in the produce aisle (such as broccoli, green beans, or broccolini).

···Tip
If the asparagus spears are on the thick side, halve them lengthwise. This reduces the cooking time considerably and ensures that the end result will be perfectly tender.

PARSLEYED CORN ON THE COB

hands-on time: 5 minutes | total time: 20 minutes | makes 6 servings

6 ears sweet corn, shucked

4 tablespoons unsalted butter, melted

$1/2$ teaspoon kosher salt

$1/4$ teaspoon black pepper

$1/4$ cup fresh flat-leaf parsley leaves, roughly chopped

Bring a large pot of water to a boil. Boil the corn until tender, 3 to 5 minutes. Drain and transfer to a serving dish. Pour the butter over the corn and sprinkle with the salt, pepper, and parsley, turning to coat. Serve with plenty of napkins.

and the next time, try...
Serving the corn in a slightly more sophisticated way: Break each ear into halves or thirds before boiling, and drizzle the cooked corn with olive oil instead of butter.

••• Tip
To rid shucked corn of its clingy, silky strands, brush a damp paper towel downward along its sides.

reliable sides

GARLIC-BUTTER BROCCOLI

hands-on time: 10 minutes | total time: 15 minutes | makes 4 servings

1 bunch broccoli (about 1 pound)
2 tablespoons unsalted butter
1 clove garlic, thinly sliced
$1/4$ teaspoon kosher salt
$1/8$ teaspoon black pepper

Bring a large pot of salted water to a boil. Meanwhile, trim the broccoli florets from the stalks. Cut the florets into small pieces. Peel the broccoli stalks and cut them crosswise into slices about $1/4$ inch thick. Cook the broccoli until almost tender but still crisp, 2 to 4 minutes. Drain; set aside. Add the butter and garlic to the empty pot and place over medium heat. Cook until the garlic is softened, 1 to 2 minutes. Add the broccoli, salt, and pepper and toss.

and the next time, try...
Turning this simple side dish into a main course by tossing it with cooked pasta.

···Tip
Broccoli florets may get all the glory, but the stalks make nice additions to a dish, too—either thinly sliced and cooked (as in this recipe) or grated and served raw (as in coleslaw). Just be sure to peel them first to remove the tough outer layer.

FENNEL SALAD

hands-on time: 20 minutes | total time: 20 minutes | makes 4 servings

1 tablespoon sour cream
1 teaspoon fresh lemon juice
3 tablespoons extra-virgin olive oil
1/2 teaspoon kosher salt
1/8 teaspoon black pepper
1 fennel bulb, cored and thinly sliced
1/2 small red onion, thinly sliced
1 red chili pepper, seeded and
   thinly sliced
1 tablespoon finely chopped
   fresh dill

Whisk together the sour cream, lemon juice, oil, salt, and black pepper in a large bowl. Add the fennel, onion, chili pepper, and dill and toss to coat. Serve immediately or cover and refrigerate for up to 5 hours.

and the next time, try...
Elevating this already elegant recipe by adding thinly sliced pears or halved red grapes.

••• Tip
You can slice the fennel using a sharp knife or a standard vegetable peeler. Or invest in a handy hand-held mandoline (available at most kitchen stores), which will make paper-thin shavings in seconds. Use it on garlic, carrots, apples, and potatoes, too.

reliable sides

MAPLE-BAKED BUTTERNUT SQUASH

hands-on time: 10 minutes | total time: 1 hour | makes 4 servings

2 2-pound butternut squashes
1 teaspoon kosher salt
4 tablespoons unsalted butter,
   cut into pieces
1/2 cup maple syrup

Heat oven to 400° F. Halve each squash lengthwise and scoop out the seeds. Place the squash halves, cut-side up, on a rimmed baking sheet or roasting pan (lined with foil for easy cleanup, if desired). Sprinkle with the salt, dot with the butter, and spoon the maple syrup over the top. Bake until softened, about 50 minutes. Let cool for a few minutes before serving.

and the next time, try...
Sweetening the squash differently. Substitute a generous sprinkle of brown sugar or a dollop of apricot jam for the maple syrup.

••• Tip
To make hard, uncooked butternut squash slightly easier to slice, microwave it for about a minute. This will soften the squash just enough to give it a little, well, give.

reliable sides

POTATO SALAD WITH GRAINY MUSTARD VINAIGRETTE

hands-on time: 15 minutes | total time: 1 hour, 30 minutes (includes marinating) | makes 8 servings

3 pounds Yukon gold potatoes
  (peel first, if desired)
1 tablespoon plus $1/2$ teaspoon
  kosher salt
$1/4$ cup fresh lemon juice
1 teaspoon honey
1 small shallot, finely chopped
2 tablespoons coarse-grain mustard
$1/2$ cup extra-virgin olive oil
$1/2$ teaspoon black pepper
1 small bunch fresh tarragon,
  chopped

Place the potatoes and 1 tablespoon of the salt in a large pot. Add enough cold water to cover. Bring to a boil. Reduce heat and simmer until the potatoes are fork-tender, about 25 minutes. Meanwhile, whisk together the lemon juice, honey, shallot, and mustard in a small bowl. Whisking constantly, slowly add the oil in a steady stream. Season with the remaining salt and $1/4$ teaspoon of the pepper; set aside. Drain the potatoes and cut them into 1-inch pieces. Transfer to a serving dish. Pour half the vinaigrette over the hot potatoes and toss. Set aside for up to 1 hour to allow the flavors to meld. Just before serving, drizzle with the remaining vinaigrette, sprinkle with the remaining pepper and the tarragon, and toss.

and the next time, try...
Giving the vinaigrette a slight crunch. Track down a coarse-grain mustard that contains whole seeds, rather than using one of the more common crushed-seed varieties.

···Tip
Pouring the vinaigrette over the potatoes while they're still hot will ensure that they really soak up the flavor.

recipe index

recipe index

recipe index

tip index

credits

MEALS MADE EASY
Food Stylist Stephana Bottom
Prop Stylist Philippa Brathwaite

REAL SIMPLE
Managing Editor Kristin van Ogtrop
Creative Director Vanessa Holden
Special Projects Editor Sarah Humphreys
Design Director, Special Projects Eva Spring
Copy Editor Myles McDonnell
Research Editor Westry Green
Food Director Frances Boswell
Food Editor Renee Schettler
Photo Editor Naomi Nista
Senior Designer Carolyn Veith Krienke
Editorial Assistant Amanda Armstrong
Recipe Tester Simon Andrews

TIME HOME ENTERTAINMENT
Publisher Richard Fraiman
Executive Director, Marketing Services Carol Pittard
Director, Retail & Special Sales Tom Mifsud
Marketing Director, Branded Businesses Swati Rao
Director, New Product Development Peter Harper
Financial Director Steven Sandonato
Assistant General Counsel Dasha Smith Dwin
Prepress Manager Emily Rabin
Book Production Manager Suzanne Janso
Product Manager Victoria Alfonso
Associate Prepress Manager
Anne-Michelle Gallero

SPECIAL THANKS TO...
Christine Austin, Jeremy Biloon, Jim Childs,
Rose Cirrincione, Lauren Hall Clark,
Jacqueline Fitzgerald, Christine Font, Jenna
Goldberg, Hillary Hirsch, Suzanne Janso,
Mona Li, Amy Mangus, Robert Marasco,
Kimberly Marshall, Amy Migliaccio, Nina Mistry,
Dave Rozzelle, Adriana Tierno, Vanessa Wu.

SPECIAL THANKS TO THE FOLLOWING STORES...
Aero, Armani Casa, Calvin Klein Home, Takashimaya.

First printing April 2006
ISBN 10: 0-8487-3815-2
ISBN 13: 978-0-8487-3815-0

We welcome your comments and suggestions about
Real Simple Books. Please e-mail us at books@realsimple.com,
or write to us at:

REAL SIMPLE BOOKS
1271 AVENUE OF THE AMERICAS
ROOM 4139
NEW YORK, NY 10020

If you would like to order any of our hardcover-edition
books, please call us at 800-327-6388 (Monday through Friday,
7:00 A.M. to 8:00 P.M. Central Time; or Saturday, 7:00 A.M.
to 6:00 P.M. Central Time).